Sartre

a biographical introduction

Sartre

a biographical introduction

Philip Thody
Professor of French Literature, University of Leeds

Charles Scribner's Sons
New York

By the same author:
Albert Camus. A study of his work (1957).
Jean-Paul Sartre. A literary and political study (1960).
Albert Camus 1913–1960 (1961).
Jean Genet. A study of his novels and plays (1968).
Jean Anouilh (1968).
Laclos : Les Liaisons Dangereuses (1970).

Now in preparation for *Leaders of Modern Thought :*
  Aldous Huxley

JUL 10 1972

The cover illustration is based on a picture supplied by The
Camera Press, London

C H

Contents

Part I

1 Childhood, literature and choice 7
2 Adolescence, manhood and philosophy 24
3 *La Nausée*, five short stories and literary criticism 41

Part II

4 The theatre, philosophy and popularity 60
5 Commitment, essays and novels 77
6 Plays, politics and villains 87

Part III

7 Communism, plays and Hungary 102
8 Colonialism, violence and tragedy 113
9 Literature, students and a conclusion 130

Bibliography 143
Notes and references 147
Selective Index 158

To Brian and Beryl Harwin

Acknowledgments

I should like to thank the staff of the Brotherton Library, University of Leeds, as well as that of the Modern Languages Library in the same University, for the help they have given me in preparing this study. Dr Howard Evans, of the University of Leeds, also drew my attention to a number of publications which I should otherwise have missed. Mrs Lorraine Winter showed exemplary care and patience in preparing the typescript for the press, while Miss Christine Bernard, of Studio Vista, saved me from writing as much about Sartre as Sartre did about Genet.

My thanks also go to my fellow tax-payers in the United Kingdom. It is their readiness to support the existence of large provincial universities with reasonable staff-student ratios which has enabled me to write this and other studies.

Part 1

1 Childhood, literature, and choice

i

Jean-Paul Charles Aymard Sartre was born in Paris on 21 June 1905. His father, Jean-Baptiste Sartre, was a naval officer and son of a country doctor from Périgord; and his mother, Anne-Marie, the only daughter and youngest child of a language teacher from Alsace, Charles Schweitzer. In 1907, Jean-Baptiste Sartre died of a fever contracted in CochinChina, and his widow was left penniless. She consequently returned, at the age of twenty, 'a tall Ariadne with a child in her arms', to live with her parents. After four years at Meudon, the family moved to 1 rue le Goff, Paris, and it was there that Sartre grew up. Anne-Marie's position was a very subordinate one – 'Families, of course, prefer widows to unmarried mothers, but only just', comments Sartre in his autobiography, *Les Mots* (1963)* – and the room which she shared with her son came to be referred to as belonging to 'the children'.[1] The most important person in the household was Charles Schweitzer, and it is he who is presented throughout *Les Mots* as having had the greatest influence on Sartre's early upbringing and subsequent career. Yet this career, as a novelist, playwright, literary critic, philosopher and political thinker, now seems to be one which Sartre wishes he had never adopted. For this reason, the portrait of Charles Schweitzer is extremely hostile, and the general account of Sartre's childhood an apparent rejection of many of the ideas which he expresses elsewhere in his work.

It would not have been surprising, given the achievements of the most famous member of the Schweitzer family, if the influence which Sartre's grandfather exercised on him had been in the field of religion. By the time Sartre was born, Albert, the son of Charles Schweitzer's younger brother Louis,[2] had already embarked on the career which was to make him into one of the foremost Protestant theologians of his day; and Sartre's own work exhibits so many features of the Protestant conscience as exemplified by Albert Schweitzer of Lambaréné that it is tempting to attribute them to a kind of intellectual or spiritual heredity. Sartre's insistence on personal responsibility, like his extreme individualism and readiness to espouse unpopular causes, his refusal of established, authoritarian modes of thought, his apparent mistrust of the body, his cult of sincerity and persistent concern for the ethical implications of human behaviour, all

* Unless otherwise stated, all quotations in this chapter are from the standard Gallimard 1964 text.

seem fundamentally Protestant. So, too, for his hostile critics, does his tendency to use literature to preach sermons, and it could even be maintained that the very titles of some of his works – *Le Diable et le Bon Dieu* (1951), *Saint Genet, Comédien et Martyr* (1952) – reflect an obsession with theological questions which is very much in the Schweitzer family tradition.

However, in 1945 Sartre defined existentialism as 'the attempt to draw all the consequences from a position of consistent atheism',[3] and his formal position has always been one of total disbelief. The one mention of Christ in his published work dismisses him in a footnote as an agitator executed by the Romans for political reasons,[4] and it would be merely perverse to argue that his evident dislike of religion reflects a need for God which he is all the more anxious to deny because he feels it so acutely. Nevertheless, given the character and achievements of Albert Schweitzer, Sartre's work often seems an inverted image of everything which his famous second cousin stood for, as well as a conscious and deliberate challenge to all forms of Christian belief. 'Bourgeois charity maintains the myth of fraternity', he wrote in 1945,[5] and his insistence that true progress now lies in the attempt of all the coloured races to liberate themselves by violence is at the furthest possible remove from Albert Schweitzer's famous remark that 'The African is my brother. But certainly my younger brother.'

If Sartre's autobiography is to be believed, the atmosphere of the Schweitzer home in which he grew up was not likely to predispose anybody towards religious faith. Charles Schweitzer had married Louise Guillemin, the daughter of a Catholic lawyer, and agreed to his children being brought up in the Catholic faith. 'Though an agnostic herself,' writes Sartre in *Les Mots*, 'Louise made them Catholic through a hatred of Protestantism', and Sartre also pointed out in 1951 how the conflict of religious faiths in the Schweitzer household had already made positive belief impossible for him before he reached the age of eleven.[6] Moreover, Charles Schweitzer was a man addicted to histrionic gestures, to the striking of noble attitudes and the transformation of everyday events into dramas where he played the leading role. Indeed, Sartre writes in *Les Mots*:

He looked so much like God the Father that he was often taken for him. One day, he entered a church through the vestry. The parish priest was warning those who were neither hot nor cold that the Lord might strike them down: 'God is here! He is watching you!', he proclaimed. Suddenly, the worshippers saw, beneath the pulpit, a tall old man with a beard, looking at them. They immediately fled. At other times when he told the story, my grandfather would say that they threw themselves at his feet. He developed a taste for such apparitions. In September 1914, he appeared in a cinema at Arcachon. We were in the circle, my mother and I, when he called for light. Other men around him were his angels, shouting out: 'Victory! Victory!'. God climbed on to the stage and read the communiqué of the battle of the Marne.

With a grandfather perpetually playing at being God, while yet having his dramatic gestures consistently undermined by the cold, nagging rationalism of his wife, it is not surprising that Jean-Paul developed little talent for religious faith. Where his grandfather did influence him was in another field, one which is analogous to religion and yet involves no faith in God: that of literature. *Les Mots* tells the story of how the peculiar situation in which Sartre found himself as a child predisposed him to accept this new and attenuated form of religious belief; how this acceptance governed the whole pattern which his life subsequently took; and how, by 1963, he had realized that the choice which he made at the age of eight or so to devote himself to literature was a mistake. Far from being, like Rousseau's *Confessions* or the autobiography of Bertrand Russell, a reasoned defence of the author's past conduct and present beliefs, it is a violent denunciation of the atmosphere in which he grew up and the effect it had on him. 'I hate my childhood, and everything that survives from it', he writes towards the end of the book, and this devastating account of the first ten and a quarter years of his life spares neither himself, his parents nor his class. Not even his own ideas on liberty, his views on the social responsibility of the writer, or the tenets of the existentialist philosophy which, in the late 1930s and early 1940s, he did so much to popularize and develop, emerge unscathed from what must be one of the most hostile accounts of his own childhood ever published by an imaginative writer.

ii

The most significant event in Sartre's early life was, of course, the death of his father. Had Jean-Baptiste survived the fever he had brought back from CochinChina, his son would not have grown up in the Schweitzer household. Anne-Marie Sartre would, in all probability, have had more children, and Jean-Paul would not have been a lonely child, with 'neither brother, sister nor friends', who spent most of his time in the imaginary world provided for him by books. More particularly, Jean-Baptiste would almost certainly have insisted that his son went regularly to school as soon as he was old enough to do so. He would not, like Charles Schweitzer, have kept Sartre at home until he was ten and a quarter, effectively cutting him off from normal contact with children of his own age, and compelling him to entertain wholly adult ideas before he was ready to do so. A theme that recurs in Sartre's work is that of sequestration, first treated in the short story 'La Chambre', published in 1939 in a collection entitled Le Mur, and further developed in two plays: Huis Clos (1944), where three people are shut up together in a very un-Christian version of Hell; and Les Séquestrés d'Altona (1959), where the hero deliberately spends thirteen years in a garret in order not to see what is happening in the outside world. When one reads Les Mots, with its portrait of a child virtually held prisoner in the top-floor flat of a building in the Latin quarter of Paris, allowed out only in the afternoons for a walk with his mother in the Luxembourg gardens, it is easy to see where the original inspiration for this theme might lie.

In his own opinion, Charles Schweitzer was keeping his grandson at home from the highest motives. Sartre had taught himself to read long before he was of an age to go to school, and was clearly something of an infant prodigy. When, on his first day at school, he was placed in the form which his grandfather considered appropriate and took down the sentence 'Le lapin sauvage aime le thym' (the wild rabbit likes thyme) as 'le lapen çovache ême le ten', it was quite clear to Charles Schweitzer that his grandson was being victimized. Rather than subject him to what he saw as the humiliation of starting off in the much lower class suited to his actual attainments, he preferred to keep Sartre away from school and have him educated 'privately'. Yet although Charles Schweitzer remained quite convinced that he was acting throughout from the highest motives, the way Sartre tells the story leaves little doubt that his grandfather was inspired by much more selfish considerations. The enthusiastic welcome which he had given Anne-Marie's child reflected, Sartre suggests, the terror which Charles Schweitzer felt at his own approaching death. The existence of his grandson, and his very presence in his house, seemed at one and the same time a gift from Heaven and a guarantee against ultimate annihilation. In choosing to keep Jean-Paul at home four or five years after the normal age at which he should have gone to school, securing him what education he could by a succession of ill-paid tutors and occasional periods at privately run academies, Charles Schweitzer was sacrificing his adored grandson's well-being to his own vanity and fear of death. In his terror that his grandson might escape from his tutelage and transfer his affection elsewhere, he effectively prevented the infant Sartre from becoming a normal child.

Sartre rightly considers his own upbringing to have been highly privileged when compared to that of a working-class orphan like Jean Genet, and writes in *Saint Genet, Comédien et Martyr* that he deeply admires the choice which Genet made to become a thief and defy society 'at an age when *we* were playing the servile buffoon'.[7] There is none the less a curious parallel between the childhood experience of the two men, and one which might explain why Sartre was so immediately sympathetic to Genet's problems when he met him in 1944. Both were the victims of a middle-class, adult society which showed no concern for their real interests, and both grew up to be writers because of the false situation in which they were placed by those officially responsible for them. The hostility which Sartre shows towards Charles Schweitzer is also connected with a number of other themes in his work, and it is interesting to see how many of the ideas expressed by a man who was, apparently, often told by his friends that he 'seemed to have had no childhood', can be traced back to what happened to him before he was ten years old.

There is, however, an obstacle to any interpretation of *Les Mots* as an autobiographical source book for Sartre's principal attitudes and ideas: the date at which it was published. An autobiography written, as Sartre revealed that *Les Mots* had been, when its author was between the ages of forty-nine and fifty-eight – he began it in 1954 and published it in review form in 1963[8] – is perhaps not the best guide to what its author really felt and thought when he was a child. Indeed, it is very much the portrait of his childhood that a middle-aged, somewhat disillusioned left-wing philosopher might be expected to give, and it would be difficult to imagine a more unromantic biography. Yet although the people and events described in *Les Mots* have obviously been passed through the sieve of Sartre's philosophical ideas and political views, the book still contains some important hints as to how he came to hold many of his later opinions. In particular, his account of how Charles Schweitzer behaved both towards Sartre himself and towards Anne-Marie is relevant to a theme which recurs in virtually every book that Sartre has published: his hostility to the middle class and his desire to see French bourgeois civilization replaced by a new society based upon socialist ideas.

Thus it is quite obvious, whether or not Sartre really thought so at the time, that his grandfather's behaviour was characteristic of the hypocrisy which almost all left-wing thinkers regard as typical of the bourgeoisie as a class. Essential to the republican ideology which Charles Schweitzer professed was the belief that all men are equal, and that the system of 'L'éducation libre, laïque et universelle' (Free, universal and lay education), established in France by the Radical Party in the 1880s, was the ideal method whereby social inequalities could be ironed out by the inevitable triumph of intelligence, ability and hard work. Given this ideology, he should have accepted either that Sartre had the intelligence to recover from his initial inability to spell, or that he would, in a democratic meritocracy, take the place assigned to him by whatever talents he possessed. Yet this was precisely what Charles Schweitzer refused to do, and one of the stories which Sartre tells about his childhood makes it quite clear that it was also through snobbery that he kept Sartre away from school. On one occasion, his 'democratic principles' demanded that he send Jean-Paul, when the family was staying at Arcachon, to the local village school. He also, however, instructed the teacher to protect 'his dearest possession' against the common herd, with the result that Jean-Paul, standing bored and dignified by the teacher's chair, realized that his 'equals', the 'sons of the people' who were officially the object of his grandfather's respect, were not regarded by Charles Schweitzer as anything but inferior and rather dangerous beings. Thanks to this attitude, Sartre was effectively protected, until he was over ten, from both the competition and the possible friendship of his equals.

It is perhaps in his description of the isolation which his grandfather's hypocrisy and selfishness forced upon him that Sartre does, after all, come nearest to what has been, since romanticism, the traditional function of literary autobiographies: the provision, in addition to an *apologia pro vita sua*, of a series of reasons why the reader should feel sorry for the author and sympathize with the sufferings he has endured. Partly because Sartre was rather small, but more particularly because he was so obviously unaccustomed to the company of his fellows, he was never accepted into any of the games organized by the other children in the Luxembourg gardens. Daily, he and his mother went for a walk there, and every day they wandered disconsolately from group to group, 'ever pleading and ever rejected'. At home, Jean-Paul was regarded by his adoring grandparents as a marvel. He had taught himself to read, he devoured the works of Corneille by himself and for his own amusement, he even wrote his own novels. But here, in the Luxembourg gardens, he discovered what he now insists was his true personality as a child: 'neither a marvel nor a medusa, but a shrimp that interested no-one'. The ostensible tone is that of Thom Gunn admiring 'All the toughs from Alexander/To those who wouldn't play with Stephen Spender', but the effect on the reader is different. The disapproval which we feel for Charles Schweitzer's dishonesty is mingled with pity for the child subjected to such indirect and unintentional humiliation, and Sartre is all the more successful in winning the reader's sympathy in that he presents himself, throughout the rest of the book, as a spoilt little boy who really rather gloried in the privileged position which the adults in his family bestowed upon him.

This neglect of his social needs as a child in not, however, the only sin which he lays at Charles Schweitzer's door. Ostensibly, his grandfather and grandmother worshipped Sartre, there was nothing they would not do for him. Yet in addition to keeping him in what was virtually a state of sequestration, they were so indifferent to his physical well-being that they did not even notice, when he was seven, that he was losing the sight of his right eye. A leucoma growing on it was to make him, he remarks in *Les Mots*, 'louche et borgne' (squinting and one-eyed) and give him that wall-eyed appearance which the literary cartoonists attracted by his later fame depict with such skill. Physical neglect coupled with over-protection is a sufficiently rare phenomenon to deserve an unusual degree of hostility, and the adult Sartre, looking back on the home where he spent his childhood, sees it as symbolic of French society as a whole during the early years of the twentieth century. While pretending to welcome their daughter back and give her a home after her husband's death, Charles and Louise Schweitzer were in fact securing the services of an unpaid domestic servant whom they exploited shamelessly:

She was not refused pocket-money: they simply forgot to give her any. When her former friends, most of them married, invited her to dinner, she had to seek permission well in advance and promise that she would be brought back before ten. Halfway through the meal, her host would have to rise from table to drive her home. Meanwhile, my grandfather, in his nightshirt, would be striding up and down the bedroom, watch in hand. On the final stroke of ten, he bellowed his disapproval. Invitations became less frequent, and my mother lost the taste for such costly pleasures.

Sartre, listening to her complaints and promising, when he grew up, to marry her and devote himself to her service, could do nothing about it at the time. But much of his subsequent political activity, and especially his consistent espousal of the interests of the exploited and oppressed, gives the impression of stemming directly from the vision he was given, when quite a young child, of the ease with which the bourgeoisie reconciles its liberal principles with both despotic and selfish practices.

There are, indeed, political overtones in many other passages of *Les Mots*, and when Charles Schweitzer declared, on receiving his royalty statement, 'Mon éditeur me vole comme dans un bois' (It's daylight robbery), Sartre writes with heavy irony that this enabled him to understand 'the exploitation of man by men'. When one remembers the genuine exploitation that

characterized all industrial societies at the beginning of the
twentieth century, it is easy to see how Sartre intends us to look
upon Charles Schweitzer as the symbol of how comical
bourgeois pretensions can be, and there is an obvious link
between the portrait of Sartre's grandfather and the bourgeois
salauds (swine) satirized in his first novel, *La Nausée* (1938).
Sometimes, sitting down to a meal, Charles Schweitzer would
look around the table and declare: 'Children, how good it is
to have nothing with which to reproach oneself'. In this respect,
of course, Sartre's dislike of the bourgeoisie is not merely
political. Protestant as well as Catholic services include the words:
'If we say we have no sin, we deceive ourselves and the truth is
not in us', and his denunciations of bourgeois hypocrisy and
self-satisfaction have a quality which recalls the diatribes which
Protestant thinkers from Calvin to Kierkegaard have hurled
against the morally complacent.

Les Mots also has other political and ideological overtones,
especially in the admiration which Sartre expresses for those
who are well integrated into the spontaneously democratic
society which, in his view, exists among children. When the
fils du peuple, in the *école communale* at Arcachon, completely
ignore the existence of this curious little boy standing in
dignified isolation by the teacher's chair, it is they and not Sartre's
grandfather who represent true democracy. Similarly, it is the
children in the Luxembourg gardens who are Sartre's 'true
equals' and against whose indifference there is no appeal. Many of
the political articles which Sartre wrote in the 1950s, and
especially *Les Communistes et la Paix* (1952-4), can be read as an
attempt to work out all the implications of a totally egalitarian
democracy in the context of modern industrialized society, and it
is perhaps significant that Sartre should, as he himself remarked,
have begun to write *Les Mots* at a time when his relationship
with the Communist Party had reached a critical stage.[9] It could
even be argued, by a hostile critic, that Sartre's enthusiasm for
the most blatantly egalitarian party in France is an attempt to
compensate himself psychologically by discovering in his adult
life something of the shared community of interests between
equals which was so lacking in his childhood, and it is a curious
feature of *Les Mots* that the book should expose him to a number
of criticisms of this kind. He is possibly even more vulnerable
in the link which this cult of equality establishes between his
early childhood and his views on religion. Throughout one of his
longest and most difficult books, *Saint Genet, Comédien et Martyr*,
he argues that the quest for sainthood is essentially a desire to
escape from the opinion of men by appealing to the higher
tribunal of God. The parallel between this interpretation of an
important aspect of the religious impulse and Sartre's own

avowed childhood tendency to seek refuge against the indifference of his equals in the admiring glances of his grandparents, is too striking to be accidental.

Les Mots does not, however, merely describe incidents which seem to show how Sartre developed many of his later philosophical and political views as a result of the tensions set up in him by his childhood. What is perhaps equally important, when one thinks of the kind of ideas which Sartre has expressed in his books, is the suggestion, never openly formulated but implied by a number of central passages in *Les Mots*, that those who are well integrated into society, who live normal, fairly conventional lives, are to be envied rather than despised; and that those who, by choice or accident, are different from their fellows, may earn our pity but cannot teach us lessons or provide us with examples to follow. Were Sartre any kind of a philosopher other than an existentialist, this would not be a particularly surprising idea to find in his autobiography. A belief in the value of ordinary experience is perfectly consistent with most traditional varieties of rationalism or empiricism, and is almost *de rigueur* in modern linguistic philosophy. In existentialism, however, it is not. However far back one traces the origins of this philosophy, its most permanent feature is an exaltation of the unusual and the irrational and a tendency to place little value on ordinary, everyday experience. Although Sartre himself is profoundly rational in many of his views, especially when he analyses anti-semitism or argues that all forms of emotion are attempts to escape from the complexity of the real world, he nevertheless shares with other existentialist thinkers a preference for the more extreme and dramatic kinds of human experience. Thus, like Pascal and Kierkegaard, he regards anguish as an emotion which reveals the true nature of man's relationship with the world and with himself. He also shares with the German philosopher Jaspers the view that the human condition reveals itself more clearly and more truly in the 'boundary situations' of fear, terror, torture and loneliness, than in normal everyday experience. Like Heidegger, he regards man as a creature cast into an absurd and incomprehensible world, with no established moral laws to guide him, no ultimate reason for his existence, and consequently no rule of right action to which he can strive to conform. In Sartre's fiction, theatre and essays, it is the characters who behave in an unusual or excessive manner whose experience is presented as important and interesting, while those who follow any kind of traditional pattern of behaviour are depicted unsympathetically. It is consequently rather surprising to find the world's leading existentialist thinker writing an autobiography which appears to regret that he was not like other children, expresses nostalgia for ordinary experience, and even casts doubts upon some of the ideas which he himself had put forward in his early work.

This nostalgia for ordinariness is most visible in the account of the way other children excluded Sartre from their games. When, eventually, he does go to school and is treated by his classmates, much to his surprise, as a quite acceptable playmate, he describes himself as being 'washed clean of the sin of existence', and this phrase is particularly significant in the light of the ideas he expressed in *La Nausée* and *L'Etre et le Néant*. Roquentin, the hero of Sartre's first novel, washes himself clean of the 'sin of existence'[10] by undertaking to write a work of art, not by taking part in any kind of communal activity and it is only in *Les Mots* that Sartre presents a conventional and communal activity such as playing games as a possibly valid refuge against anguish. Roquentin's fundamental conviction is that there is no reason for either man or the world to be as they are, or even to exist at all – an idea which Sartre refers to as 'the experience of contingency' or the 'experience of the absurd' – and this can never be dissipated by any human relationship. Virtually all Sartre's work insists on the distress which certain men legitimately feel at the realization that there is no necessity for things and people to be as they are and that their own life is given to them 'for nothing'. In *Les Mots,* this idea is mentioned only to be traced back to Sartre's own peculiar childhood and consequently devalued by being shown to have had such a highly subjective origin. Thus when he describes a recurring dream in which he is travelling in a railway compartment and cannot find his ticket, he deliberately suggests that he is worried by this problem only because his grandfather's antics have put the idea of necessity into his mind and because he suffers from the boredom of being an only child with no friends and no normal school activity to occupy him. The people whom he envies and admires, the children in the Luxembourg gardens who are 'strong and fleet of foot', are clearly never bothered by such arcane questions as whether their existence is justified or not, and are obviously quite right never to think about it. The *fils du peuple* at Arcachon are even more enviably solid and self-confident, and other passages on the same theme also have important political implications: it is only middle-class children, in their freedom from immediate and physical economic pressures, who have time to worry about such unnecessary concerns; the working-class child, besieged by hunger and the constant fear of death, 'lives in order not to die'. 'Its unjustifiable condition justifies its existence'; and it has no time for metaphysical problems.

Like a number of ideas expressed in *Les Mots*, this apparent rejection of the fundamental presuppositions in Sartre's early existentialism is not without its ambiguities. Charles Schweitzer is wrong to be a self-satisfied bourgeois who never asks any questions about himself; but he is equally wrong to have reached the stage of thinking in the very terms of necessity and contingency on which Sartre's own philosophy depends. It is also clear, on a little reflection, that the absorption of the working class in their immediate needs merely postpones the moment when they too will ask about the whys and wherefores, and in this respect Antoine Roquentin is a keener thinker than his creator. He is quite aware that people cannot immerse themselves permanently in one particular activity, and will have to keep looking for new diversions to hide 'the enormous absurdity of their existence' from themselves.[11] Moreover, Sartre's own position in which, as he says in *Les Mots*, he was not 'stable and permanent . . . not necessary to the fabrication of steel', stemmed directly from the fact that he had no father, and his views on fatherhood are perhaps the most ambiguous aspect of the book.

Sometimes, he says he was glad Jean-Baptiste disappeared so early. 'By restoring Anne-Marie to her chains', he writes, this disappearance 'gave me my liberty'; and the appearance so early in his autobiography of the key word in Sartre's philosophy gives the initial impression that he is going to present himself as a kind of hero. He will be the child whose experience prefigures that of all the characters in his novels and plays who discover that they too are free, and this impression is confirmed when Sartre goes on to write: 'If he had lived, my father would have lain down full length upon me and crushed me. Fortunately, he died young. Among the Aeneases each carrying his Anchises on his shoulders, I cross the seas alone, detesting those invisible fathers riding piggy-back upon their sons throughout their lives.' The view that all fathers dominate and possess their sons, straddling their necks as the Old Man of the Sea rode upon Sinbad, and injecting their authoritarian ideas into them as Anchises did into the pious Aeneas, recurs in *Les Séquestrés d'Altona*, written at the time when Sartre was working upon *Les Mots*, and is also central to the long extracts which he published between 1957 and 1967 of his forthcoming essay on Flaubert. It is clearly an idea to which Sartre attaches considerable importance, and which is fully consistent with his anti-authoritarian attitude towards society. When he says that he agrees with an eminent psychiatrist that he has 'no super-ego', he clearly indicates that he is rather pleased with what happened, and in this respect the opening pages in *Les Mots* suggest that it is only because Sartre lost his father at such an early age that he was able to develop a philosophy which gives pride of place to the essentially human quality of freedom.

Yet while the absence of a father gave Sartre his freedom, it also deprived him of the self-assurance which even nowadays he finds rather enviable in other people. Thus he tells how he recently went into a restaurant and was struck by the behaviour of 'the proprietor's son, a little boy of seven', who shouted to the cashier: 'When my father isn't here, I'm the Master'. Sartre's comment on this incident is: 'There's a man for you! When I was his age, I was nobody's master and nothing belonged to me', and it is a remark which seems to be made without any ironic intent. A few pages later on, he tells a story of how he made a fool of himself when taking part in some amateur dramatics with a group of other children, and it is clear that he did so only because he was unaccustomed to the society of his equals and unable to adjust to a situation where he had rivals for the adults' attention. This incident, like his evocation of himself as a forlorn, unhappy child excluded by his fellows from their games, reinforces the impression given by the tone of his autobiography taken as a whole: what Sartre would really like to have been was not a peculiar little boy who grew up to be a famous writer, but a member of a large, vigorous, probably working-class family, kept firmly in his place by a father of granitic solidity, and compelled to learn equality and democracy from the very beginning in the ordinary rough and tumble of family life.

Yet he could have done this only if Jean-Baptiste Sartre had survived, and on almost the same page that he describes the incident in the restaurant, he speaks in very different terms of just how his father would have influenced him if he had lived. To write 'creating my principles from his moods, my knowledge from his ignorance, my pride from his rancour and my laws from his manias' is not the most obvious way of expressing regret for an absent father, and the phrase seems rather to indicate that Sartre is pleased to have grown up with adults whom he was never tempted to take seriously. For as he makes clear, when describing Charles Schweitzer as the 'victim of two recently discovered techniques: the art of photography and *L'Art d'être Grandpère*', his grandfather spent most of his time playing a part. With Jean-Paul, it was precisely that of a grandfather, and the famous analysis in *L'Etre et le Néant* of the waiter who 'plays at being a waiter'[12] in order better to realize what he is, may perhaps owe something to Sartre's childhood memories. Another result of Charles Schweitzer's general behaviour was also to imbue both his grandson and the rest of the household with his own taste for play-acting, so that all Jean-Paul knew of reality was its 'laughing inconsistency'; and it is perhaps by reaction against this atmo- sphere that Sartre imagines real fathers as endowed with such irresistible authority, attributing his uncertainty about the kind of person he was to his grandfather's normally irresponsible and histrionic behaviour. But on one occasion, Charles Schweitzer did

suddenly take on a different aspect. He acted as Sartre thinks real
fathers tend to act, and determined his grandson's future for him.

iii

After Sartre had taught himself to read, it was a relatively short
step for him to begin writing his own books. He had little else to
do, and lived in a house where literature enjoyed great official
respect. After all, the family lived not only from what Charles
Schweitzer earned as a teacher but also from the royalties which
came in from his books. When Sartre wrote out his own stories,
he naturally evoked rounds of applause, and the imaginary world
he created for himself served as a convenient refuge against the
disappointments he encountered elsewhere. Without the intervention of Charles Schweitzer, all this might have remained
simply a game. It is not, though Sartre himself does not mention
it, so uncommon for lonely children to seek refuge and
consolation by reading books or even by writing their own.
Later on, when they start to lead a more normal life, they forget
all about it. What gave Sartre's experience its crucial importance
in his later development was not, according to *Les Mots*, a
particularly acute attack of loneliness but a sudden change in his
grandfather's behaviour and attitude. For once, he ceased to be
an amiable buffoon and spoke to Sartre seriously, like a father to
his son, warning him of the dangers accompanying the literary
career which he seemed likely to adopt. Sartre comments,
underlining the crucial importance of the episode:

> If Charles had cried out, seeing me in the distance, 'Here is
> our new Hugo; behold the budding Shakespeare!' I should
> now be an industrial designer or a sixth-form master. No
> danger of that. For the first time, I was face to face with the
> Patriarch. He seemed morose, and all the more venerable
> because he had forgotten to worship me. It was Moses
> dictating the new Law. My Law. He had mentioned my
> vocation only to underline its disadvantages; I assumed that
> he regarded it as already decided.

What is particularly interesting about this incident, when
considered in the light of Sartre's later ideas, is the way it
coincides with some of the presuppositions of what he himself
calls, in *L'Etre et le Néant*, 'existential psychoanalysis'.[13]
According to this technique of studying human behaviour, it is
some time between the ages of seven and ten that children decide
on the kind of person they are going to be when they grow up.
It was when Sartre was about eight or nine that this incident
took place, and the three other people to whom he has applied

the methods of existential psychoanalysis are all presented as
having made their 'basic choice' at about the same age. Charles
Baudelaire was seven and a half when his widowed mother married
Major Aupick and thus led her son to take what Sartre presents
as a conscious decision to become a 'misunderstood child'.
It is when Jean Genet is about eight that he begins to steal small
objects from his foster-parents and, caught in the act, consciously
declares: 'I will be a thief';[14] and it is when Gustave Flaubert is
seven or eight that his father abruptly ceases to treat him as
a treasured and favourite object, plunging him into a situation
where he 'interiorizes' this rejection and feels such shame that
he 'begins scratching the earth to dig the hole where he will be
able to hide himself from everyone'.[15]

Until the mid 1950s, when his increasing sympathy with
Marxism led him to start attributing more and more importance
to the effect which social environment has on individual character,
Sartre insisted that the choices which people made were always
free. In L'Etre et le Néant, he argued that even the man who is
being tortured still remains free to decide whether to talk or not,
since he alone decides when the point has come at which he can
bear the pain no longer; and even as late as 1952, in Saint Genet,
Comédien et Martyr, he insisted that sexual tastes resulted
from a kind of choice and were not caused by either physiological
or environmental factors.[16] In the context of these arguments,
Sartre himself could be considered as having made, 'between the
ages of eight and ten', a free choice to become a writer. After all,
such a choice would have been a fairly obvious one for a child
living in a house dominated by books and anxious to make sense
of his experience by integrating himself into the values held by the
rest of the family. In this respect, Les Mots does initially seem to
illustrate some of the basic tenets of Sartre's first version of
existentialism, and to be an example of existential psychoanalysis.

A closer study of the text, however, shows a number of
significant changes in Sartre's attitude. Jean Genet's choice
to be a thief and become something like the living embodiment
of evil is depicted by Sartre as a conscious process which,
although starting when he was about nine, continued right
through his adolescence. Similarly, the whole of Baudelaire's
conduct is presented as the deliberate prolongation of the decision
taken when his mother remarried. In Sartre's own case, on the
other hand, everything is quite different. When he is about ten
and a quarter the choice goes underground, and he apparently
forgets all about it. Moreover, there seems to be very little that he
could have done either then or later to alter the pattern which
this choice was to impose upon his life, and there is in this
respect a particularly important difference between Les Mots and
Baudelaire.

Implicit in Sartre's highly moralistic approach to Baudelaire is the idea that someone who has taken a 'wrong' choice can reform. 'The least thing, a change of mind, a mere look into the eyes of these idols would have been enough to make his chains fall at once to the ground', he writes of Baudelaire's highly respectful attitude towards the official authorities of his day,[17] and this remark is fully in keeping with his initial thesis that people think and behave only as they choose, and not in accordance with external compulsion, biological necessity, Pavlovian conditioning or unalterable early choice. In *Les Mots*, however, this presupposition disappears. Sartre's original choice may have been free, but once it had been made its effects became inescapable. At the end of the book, discussing the disillusionment which he now feels with literature in general and with his own 'vocation' in particular, he writes: 'Moreover, this old ruined house, my imposture, is also my character: you can get rid of a neurosis; you are never cured of yourself. All the characteristics of the child, worn, defaced, humiliated, huddled in a corner and passed over in silence, have survived in the fifty-year old man.' A grandfather's momentary lapse into gravity can produce effects just as inescapable as those stemming from a father's more consistent tyranny. From one's childhood, there is no escape.

It is in this dismissal of the more optimistic view of human freedom which had informed all Sartre's early work that the philosophical implications of *Les Mots* echo his general disillusionment with literature and the regret which he seems to feel that he ever became a writer at all. At the end of the book, in an apparent rejection of the ideas which he had put forward in the 1940s on the need for writers to take sides in politics, he writes: 'For a long time, I treated my pen as a sword: now I realize how helpless we are. It does not matter. I am writing, I shall write books; they are needed; they have a use all the same. Culture saves nothing and nobody, nor does it justify. But it is a product of man: he projects himself through it and recognizes himself in it; this critical mirror alone shows him his image.' The hope which informed *Qu'est-ce que la Littérature?*, in 1947, was that books would be the self-consciousness of a society in permanent revolution, influencing the way men behaved by pointing out to them the tasks which had to be performed. This now seems to have gone, and the only thing which literature now offers is the purely passive image which man obtains by seeing himself in a looking-glass.

The idea of commitment in literature (*la littérature engagée*) was not, however, one of the ideas inculcated into Sartre by his grandfather. The Protestant conscience and religious vocation of the Schweitzers had, in Charles, assumed the guise of a belief in a very different kind of literature from the one which his grandson was to make famous in the 1940s. An eminent French critic once said that the nineteenth century 'began with the poetry of religion and ended with the religion of poetry', and it was more than a semi-religious concept of literature that Charles Schweitzer both entertained himself and transmitted to his grandson. In it, according to *Les Mots*:

> ... the earth was the prey of Evil, and there was only one salvation: to die to oneself and to the World, and from the depths of this shipwreck to contemplate the unattainable Ideas. Since no-one could succeed in this without a hard and dangerous training, the task had been entrusted to a body of specialists. The clergy took charge of humanity and saved it by the reversibility of merits: the wild beasts of the temporal world, great and small, had ample leisure in which to kill one another, or to lead a stultified, inauthentic existence, since writers and artists meditated on their behalf on Beauty and Goodness. To tear the entire human race away from its animal state, only two conditions had to be fulfilled: that the relics of dead clerics – paintings, books, statues – should be preserved in supervised premises; and that at least one living cleric should remain to carry on the task and manufacture future relics.

If there is one thing for which Sartre is famous, it is his argument that the writer should come down from his ivory tower and concern himself with the things of this world; and the most extraordinary feature of *Les Mots* is that he should claim to have held on to this religious vision of the artist's calling until about 1952 or 1953. This is surely what he must mean when he writes at the end of the volume that for 'ten years now' he has 'been like a man waking up from a dream, cured of a long, bitter-sweet madness', and he did in fact confirm in an interview in 1964 that he had made no error of dating in this part of his autobiography.[18] The books he has actually published are so completely different from the description of the writer's calling in *Les Mots* that it is almost as if someone who has just made a fortune on the Stock Exchange were suddenly to claim that he had been inspired throughout by the doctrines of St Francis of Assisi. One of the major problems which any biography of Sartre has to confront is consequently that of trying to see how *Baudelaire, Les Mains Sales* and *Qu'est-ce que la Littérature?* could possibly have been written by a man convinced in his heart of hearts that literature had to concern itself with eternal aesthetic values. It is not a problem which can be easily solved, and the only possible way of linking Sartre's actual literary career with what he says about his literary ambitions in *Les Mots* is to see it as a constant if not always conscious struggle against the ideas he absorbed as a child.

He did, after all, say in 1969 that he had always written the very
opposite of what he wanted to write,[19] and one of the many
paradoxes of *Les Mots* is that the ambitions it describes should
have been fulfilled in a way that Sartre claims he never expected.
If he does not carry the description of his childhood beyond the
point where he first went regularly to school, it is perhaps
because he considered, in 1963, that everything important and
formative had already happened to him before he was eleven. A
study of his life from the beginning of the academic year 1915–16
will show how seriously this idea may be taken.

2 Adolescence, manhood and philosophy

Sartre was ten and a quarter when, as he puts it in *Les Mots*, his grandparents 'could not think of keeping him sequestred any longer' and entered him as a day boy in the junior Lycée Henri IV. Initially, as might be expected, he did not do very well, and it was only after his mother had persuaded his form master to 'keep an eye' on him that Sartre, convinced that the lessons were intended for him alone and that he had therefore not lost his unique position in the eyes of the adult world, began to improve. By the end of the year, he had learned to accept the *ex cathedra* teaching addressed to everyone, and thus, as he says, 'grown used to democracy'. Moreover, 'adopted from the very first as if it were the most natural thing in the world', he had friends with whom he could play as an equal among equals. It was then that he really 'washed himself clean of the family comedy', and felt his dreams of literary glory to be 'morbid and insipid' by the side of the 'lightning intuitions' which he gained through play.

This exchange of his solitary life in his grandparents' flat for the healthier atmosphere of ordinary school life was not, however, the only change which came over Sartre at that period. In 1916, when he was eleven, his mother remarried. His stepfather, a M. Mancy, was Comptroller of the La Rochelle dockyards and, like the Jean-Baptiste Sartre whose portrait then disappeared from above Anne-Marie's bed, a graduate of one of the engineering schools established in France at the beginning of the nineteenth century. Simone de Beauvoir describes Sartre, in the late 1920s, as regarding the word 'engineer' as the final and most crushing insult in his vocabulary, and he certainly seems to have had an imperfect sympathy for his stepfather. According to Francis Jeanson, a writer and political journalist much influenced by Sartre's ideas, and author of one of the few studies of him to have received Sartre's blessing, Sartre experienced nothing of the hatred which Baudelaire felt for Major Aupick when Madame Baudelaire remarried,[1] and this fits in with a number of remarks which Sartre makes about his attitude towards Anne-Marie. Since he had no rival for his mother's affection and interest between the ages of three and five, the period which Freud regards as essential in a boy's relationship with his parents, he developed no Oedipus complex and, so he asserts, 'no aggressiveness either'. While it is difficult to take this remark quite at its face value – Philip Toynbee, reviewing the English translation of *Les Mots* in 1964 said with

some justification that he found it 'an incredibly aggressive book'
– it does seem that Sartre was not thrown into paroxysms of
despair at having to share Anne-Marie with someone else. If
his account of the basic crisis in his childhood is correct, there
would indeed have been few areas of friction between him and
M. Mancy. Everything important had already happened to him
by the time he had entered his teens, and the one reference which
he has so far made to his stepfather in his published works is,
although not flattering, very different from the violent attacks
which he makes on Charles Schweitzer throughout *Les Mots*.
'I lived for ten years under the sway of a polytechnicien', he
wrote of M. Mancy in 1960. 'He killed himself with work – or,
rather, somewhere in Paris, his work had decided that it would
kill him. He was the shallowest of men. On Sundays, he would
withdraw into himself, find a desert, and feel lost. He clung on,
however, saved by somnolence – or by attacks of anger inspired by
vanity. Fortunately, by then, the war had broken out. He read the
newspapers, cutting out articles and sticking them in the pages
of an exercise book.'[2]

The tone is one of rather pitying tolerance for the technocrats
who allow themselves to be caught up in the power structure
of a managerial society, but it does also indicate that it was not
only Sartre's poor mathematics which prevented him from
following both his father's and his stepfather's example and
entering an *école polytechnique*. Instead, he specialized on the
arts side, and left the Lycée at La Rochelle in 1919 in order to
return to the Lycée Henri IV in Paris. Marc Beigbeder, one of
his earliest biographers, suggests that this move was aimed at
removing Sartre from some rather unhealthy adolescent contacts,
and mentions the short story *L'Enfance d'un Chef* as providing
supplementary evidence of this. Sartre's two most recent
biographers, Michel Contat and Michel Rybalka, also state that
he was very unhappy in his teens, and that he stole books and
sums of money from his mother and stepfather. Another possible
explanation for this move, however, is that the philosopher and
writer Alain had been teaching at Henri IV since 1909 and was
well launched on a career during which he was to impart his own
version of Cartesian rationalism on a whole generation who
attended his classes. Sartre was already showing promise on the
literary and philosophical side. A move to Paris, where he could
also stay with relatives while attending courses at Henri IV, was
a natural step. It was, after all, what all young Frenchmen of
his age, interests and social background would do.

In 1924, Sartre won a place in the competitive examination
for entry into the Ecole Normale Supérieure de la rue d'Ulm,
the most select and intellectual of all French institutions of
higher education. It accepts only a limited number of students,

allows them to live in, and encourages them to do most of their
work in small groups, with only occasional consultation with
their lecturers and tutors. Contrasting his own privileged
situation with that of the average French student of 1968,
Sartre later described himself as having studied in an atmosphere
of 'aristocratic leisure', completely shielded from the overcrowding
and neglect which even then characterized much French
university education. During one academic year, apparently,
he and his fellow students from the rue d'Ulm went to a lecture
at the Sorbonne only once, and then solely to show support for a
professor whose lectures were being boycotted by right-wing
student groups.[3] After five years at the Ecole Normale Supérieure,
Sartre was successful in his second attempt at the *Agrégation de
Philosophie*, the competitive examination whereby philosophy
teachers are recruited for the *lycées*. He then had to spend
eighteen months in the army, and did his national service in the
meteorological section.

The major source for any account of Sartre's life from 1929
onwards is the three volumes of Simone de Beauvoir's
autobiography, and especially the second two, *La Force de l'Age*
(1960) and *La Force des Choses* (1963). It is difficult to discover
from this autobiography when certain events took place, but
it is nevertheless fairly clear that she met Sartre in 1928 or 1929,
and became his mistress not very long afterwards. She was a
student of philosophy at the Sorbonne at the same time that
Sartre was at the rue d'Ulm, and the first actual mention of him
in her book refers to the surprise which everybody felt when he
failed to do well enough in the written paper of the *Agrégation*
to qualify for the oral. It took her some time to get to know him,
and penetrate into the group to which he belonged, one composed
of 'former pupils of Alain renowned for its brutality'.[4] Sartre, in
fact, was rumoured to be the worst of the lot and even to Drink,
and it was not until she had already struck up a friendship with
a milder member of the group, André Herbaud, that she came into
contact with him. In 1929, Sartre came first and Simone de
Beauvoir second in the *Agrégation de Philosophie* and from that
point onwards their lives have tended, for all their refusal to
commit themselves to the bourgeois institution of marriage, to
coincide almost as completely as those of man and wife.

Her first description of Sartre's personality, habits and ambitions
bears out the accuracy of his portrait of his childhood in *Les Mots*
in one obviously important and one apparently minor way.
Almost from the very beginning, she notes that it was indeed a
form of salvation that he was seeking in literature, and she
summarizes what was to become one of the important themes in
Qu'est-ce que la Littérature? in 1947 when she writes that he
regarded himself as having received a mandate to 'bear witness

for all things and assume them on his own account in the light of necessity'.[5] The idea that the writer can rescue the world from ordinariness by giving it a necessary, as distinct from accidental, existence recurs in a different form in the closing passages of *La Nausée* in 1938, and the Sartre of the 1930s does seem, in this respect, to be the prolongation of the little boy who spent his days at 1, rue le Goff dreaming about becoming a great writer. In 1964, Sartre remarked how Simone de Beauvoir had recognized that his conduct was governed by a conviction that he must become a writer, and had done so long before he realized that this was the driving force behind everything he did. What is peculiar to a neurosis, he stated, is that it presents itself to the person suffering from it as being the most natural thing in the world, and it was only much later that he himself came to understand the nature of his 'long bitter-sweet madness'.[6]

Early in their relationship, Sartre also took Simone de Beauvoir to the open-air bookstalls on the banks of the Seine and bought her copies of *Pardaillan* and *Fantômas*, commenting as he did so on how much he preferred them to the recently published correspondence between Alain Fournier and Jacques Rivière. As he remarks in *Les Mots*, they had been his staple diet and genuinely favourite reading during his childhood, and it is clear that the taste for them had not left him. He himself hints, in his autobiography, that the frequency with which the heroes in these comics rescued maidens in distress and saved kingdoms from ruin left him with a permanent taste for epic achievements; there is also perhaps another aspect of his work that can be attributed to them: the feeling which he clearly has that he must always place himself on the side of the oppressed. On a more amusing but perhaps more significantly philosophical level, the preference which he expressed to Simone de Beauvoir for the lowbrow *Fantômas* over the highbrow Fournier can already be found in *Les Mots* in the remarks that he still prefers the American style thrillers of the *Série Noire* to the works of Wittgenstein. It is a confession which the reader of his works on the imagination might be tempted to take with a grain of salt.

Simone de Beauvoir does not, however, in any way limit her description of Sartre to his literary ambitions. We learn about his desire to travel, and note with a certain amusement that his early dreams of vast voyages to far-away places sound like a first version of the globe-trotting which the Roquentin of *La Nausée* found so disappointing.[7] We discover how his anarchistic attitude towards society was so totally apolitical that he never even took the trouble to vote in any elections. We read about his experiments with mescalin, which produced not the ecstatic visions vouchsafed to Aldous Huxley but only horrific visions of 'des crabes, des poulpes, des choses grimaçantes' (crabs,

octopuses, grimacing things). While recognizing them as
hallucinations, he also felt afraid that the time would come when
he was genuinely convinced that 'a lobster was trotting behind
him'. Later on, he apparently did feel that one was following him
all one night as he walked round Venice. Peter Green, the
English translator of *La Force de l'Age* (*The Prime of Life*), once
maintained in a very amusing correspondence in the *Observer*
that the crabs and other shellfish were all a myth invented by
Sartrè as an excuse not to accompany Simone de Beauvoir on the
long walks which she insisted on taking in the country, and this
would fit in with his lack of enthusiasm for the natural scenery
occasionally described in his novels.[8] However, the ordering of
events in the rest of *La Force de l'Age* does not really bear this out.
Even after the mescalin experience had introduced Sartre to the
shellfish which were later to provide him with such interesting
imagery in *Les Séquestrés d'Altona*, he still went on a walking
tour with her in the area near the Gorges du Tarn. On a later
occasion, it is true, he refused to accompany her on the ascent
of Mount Taygetus, in Greece. But then he needed no hallucinations to justify his refusal. The climb took nine and a half
hours and the temperature was in the eighties.

Existentialism has frequently been defined in terms of the
attention which it pays to immediate, day to day experience, and
it is fully within the conventions of this philosophy that Simone
de Beauvoir should write so much about her own and Sartre's
private and even trivial experiences. She tells us that he so
enjoyed smoking a pipe that when tobacco was in short supply
during the Occupation, he picked dog-ends up from off the
pavement; that he was a good swimmer, but always felt nervous
lest an octopus might reach out one of its tentacles and pull him
down into the depths of the sea; that his dislike of Titian, basic
to the aesthetic expressed in his later essay on Tintoretto *Le
Séquestré de Venise*, dated from his earliest visits to Italy; that
he spoke German without an accent; that he was fond of jazz
and the cinema, and had a special liking for the Marx brothers
films; that he had an attractive bass voice and could give a good
rendering of *Ol' Man River*; and that he was so overwhelmed by
Al Jolson singing *Sonny Boy* that he cried. Naturally, little of
Simone de Beauvoir's account of his life during the thirties
and early forties is as disconnected as the above summary makes
it sound. Even the passing references to the visits which Sartre
paid to his parents, accompanying them on a cruise to Norway
and going to see them at their home in the elegant suburb of
Passy, indicate that he remained on fairly good terms with them,
and had not broken off all personal contact with the better
sections of the middle class so violently attacked in his novels.
Other anecdotes are even more significant, as when she describes

two of Sartre's reactions to a violent attack of renal colic some time in the thirties. In the first place, he told the doctor that 'suffering is porous', and thus anticipated one of the major themes of *L'Être et le Néant*: because he is always conscious of what he is and what he feels, man can never coincide absolutely with his being or his emotions.[9] And in the second, he went on to argue, in an impeccably Kiplingesque manner, that 'If you gave way to tears, to nervous upsets, to sea-sickness, then it was because you weren't really trying'. It is when we read, in *L'Etre et le Néant*, that the person who chooses to give way to his fatigue on a long walk thereby reveals the free project which he has made both of himself and of his relationship to his body,[10] that we realize how much of Sartre's philosophy can be seen as an extrapolation of his own personal attitudes and an attempt to evolve a kind of 'life style' for himself as well as for other people.

However, it is naturally Simone de Beauvoir's more general account of Sartre's early philosophical and literary attitudes which is of most interest, and her description of the fascination which objects exercised over him is a very good introduction to any study of the inter-relationship between Sartre and the phenomenology of Husserl. Neither is she alone in dispelling the illusion that Sartre was the gloomy, morbidly neurotic social misfit popularly supposed to have drawn his own self-portrait in *La Nausée* or *L'Age de Raison*. Those who, in the 1930s, were privileged to meet him on the terrace of La Coupole, in Montmartre, saw a young man very different from Antoine Roquentin or even Mathieu Delarue. He was lively, witty, irreverent, an excellent companion, and a particularly appreciative connoisseur of the young ladies who chose La Coupole as a place to display their charms.[11] Similarly, the Sartre who appeared at first sight to have written a masterpiece with his very first novel, achieving success overnight with the publication of *La Nausée* without any painful apprenticeship, had in fact been working on the themes expressed in this novel for at least six years before finally discovering an artistic form suited to them.

ii

Sartre's first excursion into the literary world did not, in fact, actually see the light of day until about forty years after he had written it. On 7 January 1950, *Le Figaro Littéraire* published a letter which Sartre had written to the humorous novelist and playwright Georges Courteline on the occasion of Courteline's promotion to a higher rank in the *Légion d'Honneur* in 1910. Courteline did not reply, and Sartre thinks that he was quite right not to do so, dismissing the incident in *Les Mots* as yet another example of how Charles Schweitzer encouraged him to

adopt a ridiculously precocious attitude in his relationships with
other people. 'En écrivant à l'enfant, il serait tombé sur le grandpère', is Sartre's own, and probably accurate, assessment of the
situation. But at the time, the Schweitzer family judged him
harshly. 'Hang it all, you reply to a *child*', was Charles's indignant
comment.

The histrionic talent which Charles Schweitzer so delighted to
employ in order to give added interest to everyday occasions
clearly left Sartre with a taste for play acting, and he commented
on this in his notes on Francis Jeanson's study of him in the
Ecrivains par Eux-mêmes series in 1955. When he was a student
at the Ecole Normale Supérieure de la rue d'Ulm in the 1920s,
he wrote the texts for a number of annual revues. These included
the neo-Proustian *A l'Ombre des Vieilles Billes en Fleurs* as well
as *Le Désastre de Langson,* in which he impersonated the renowned
literary historian, Gustave Lanson.[12] However, none of these texts
has survived, and his first published work was all in prose. An
extract entitled *L'Ange du Morbide* appeared in an ephemeral
review entitled *La Revue sans titre* in 1923 and tends to confirm
the accuracy of his subsequent description of himself at the time
as a 'clumsy hunter after adjectives'.[13] It describes an incident in
the life of a school-teacher with the rather inappropriate name of
Louis Gaillard, who had 'turned the whole of his youthful
ardour, through snobbery, towards the morbid side of life'.
Louis, a somewhat perverse and even perverted early version
of Antoine Roquentin, is attempting to seduce a girl suffering
from tuberculosis, but suddenly finds the idea of being infected
with this disease overwhelmingly horrible when he tries to kiss
her. Reassured by a plethora of specialists that he has not been
infected, he marries 'une Alsacienne rose, blonde, bête et saine'
(a fair-haired, rosy-cheeked, stupid and healthy girl from Alsace)
and gives up literature. At the age of fifty-five, he receives the
Légion d'Honneur, 'brevet incontesté de bourgeoisie' (an
undisputed badge of middle-class respectability), a decoration
which Sartre himself was to refuse, in company with Albert Camus,
at the end of the last war.[14]

The *Revue sans Titre* was edited by Sartre's friend Paul Nizan,
already at that time, according to Sartre, an accomplished writer,
and a person for whom Sartre has always expressed the greatest
admiration. It was also Nizan who arranged for an extract of
Sartre's essay '*La Légende de la Vérité*' to appear in the slightly
more firmly established review *Bifur* in 1930, and who described
his friend, in a note at the end of the volume, as a young
philosopher 'preparing a volume of destructive philosophy'
('Jeune philosophe. Prépare un volume de philosophie destruct-
rice'). In fact, the published extract from '*La Légende de la
Vérité*' is not all that destructive. It anticipates *La Nausée,* a

much more violently expressed and subversive work, by arguing that man finds in nature only the regular laws which he puts there himself, and that language expresses the categories of man's mind rather than the reality of the external world. The very idea of truth, Sartre maintains, arose only when man began to trade with his fellows, and it was an unnatural concept from the beginning. It did, however, give rise to democracy and to the rule of law. Only people who accepted that they were free and equal could agree to settle their differences by an appeal to the impartial tribunal of truth rather than to the whim of a tyrant.[15]

Between 1928 and 1929, according to Simone de Beauvoir, Sartre had written a novel called *Une défaite*, based on the love affair between Nietzsche and Cosima Wagner, and it is clear that he was oscillating, throughout the late twenties and early thirties, between fiction and the essay as the best medium for his ideas. It was the publication of Céline's *Voyage au bout de la nuit* in 1930 which apparently made him decide to abandon what Simone de Beauvoir calls the 'style gourmé' (pompous style) which he had used in *'La Légende de la Vérité'*, and to effect a more rigid separation between straightforward philosophical exposition on the one hand and fiction on the other. His directly philosophical preoccupations were to lead, in 1936, to the publication of his first article, *'La Transcendance de l'Ego'*, in the 'establishment' philosophical journal, *Recherches philosophiques,* as well as to the publication of his first book, *L'Imagination,* later in the same year. At the same time, he was reworking some of the ideas first expressed in *'La Légende de la Vérité'*, mingling them with occasional but ironic reminiscences of the Gaillard of *L'Ange du Morbide,* and mixing in some more amusing reflections on provincial life as he had seen it in Le Havre and La Rochelle. The result was to be *La Nausée*, the fictional *summa* of his major pre-war ideas, and a decisive move away from technical philosophy and literature as a spare-time occupation.

iii

On several occasions in *Les Mots*, Sartre evokes the vision of his future which his grandparents' view of the world and his own early literary ambitions used to give him of his future: that of a sixth-form master who teaches Greek during the day and devotes his spare time to composing delicate monographs describing the monuments of Aurillac. Mathieu Delarue, the semi-autobiographical hero of *Les Chemins de la Liberté* (published between 1945 and 1949, consisting of *L'Age de Raison, Le Sursis* and *La Mort dans l'Ame*) refers to himself at one point as a 'Sunday writer'[16] – a comparison with the *peintres du dimanche* who compensate for the

drabness of their ordinary lives by spending Sunday painting
water-colours – and Sartre's official career between 1929 and the
outbreak of World War II was very much that of a philosophy
teacher who used his spare time to write books. As an *agrégé*, the
highest grade in the French schoolteaching profession, he did
have plenty of spare time, since his contract would have obliged
him to teach only about twelve hours a week, and the portrait
which Simone de Beauvoir gives of him does not indicate that he
was over-worked. When he was officially teaching at Le Havre,
he managed to spend most of his time in Paris, and in 1936 he
turned down the prospect of promotion to a senior post at Lyons
and took an apparently less interesting one at Laon. The reason
was that the post at Laon would enable him to spend every
vacation and week-end in Paris, as well as going there at least
once a week even during term time. Although Bouville (mud-
town) is said to be based on Le Havre, where Sartre taught from
1931 to 1936, both he and Simone de Beauvoir liked the town,
and preferred it to Rouen, where she too was teaching in the
local *lycée*, and finding the Normandy middle class rather narrow-
minded. Sartre was apparently much appreciated as a teacher,
though a shade eccentric by the normal standards of French
academic life. He never wore a collar and tie, and would
occasionally break off the lesson he was giving in order to remark
upon how the absurdity of existence had suddenly overwhelmed
him. When asked to give a speech at the *Distribution Solennelle
des Prix* at Le Havre in 1931, he chose what was then the rather
daring and unusual subject of the cinema.[17]

He nevertheless seems to have been very successful in what
many people consider to be the essential task of a philosophy
teacher: that of encouraging his pupils to call into question all
their preconceived ideas. One of the anecdotes which he told
in 1968 about his early career is also an interesting reflection of
the insistence which he had always placed, in his books, on the
importance of argument and contestation. When he was
appointed to Laon, in 1936, he found his pupils totally convinced
of the reality of the external world and completely unaware that
anyone might ever call it into question. He consequently spent
the first month telling them about Kantian idealism and the
view that 'the so-called reality of the external world is constituted
by the internal unity of our own experiences'. When they at
last declared, after a fierce resistance, 'We've understood', their
grasp of the idea was all the more certain and all the more
satisfying because of their initial resistance. In contrast, the
sophisticated pupils whom he had to teach later in his career,
when he moved to the Lycée Pasteur, in Paris, could learn
nothing. The newspapers and radio had given them a set
of fashionable but totally superficial ideas about psychology

and philosophy which made them quite incapable of genuine argument. Consequently, at the end of the year, they had made no progress.[18]

Sartre had been appointed to the Lycée Pasteur in 1937, after only one year in the academic wilderness at Laon, and a journalist writing in *Les Nouvelles Littéraires* in 1938, after Sartre had begun to attain a certain reputation in literary circles, told how he had overheard two of his pupils talking about him in a bookshop.[19] He was, apparently, known as 'Sartrus', and was said to be very good in the lessons which he gave on André Gide, then still regarded by the French establishment as a dangerously advanced thinker. The fact that Sartre had moved in eight years – with one year's leave of absence in Berlin – from provincial exile to the academic Mecca of Paris is an indication that his slightly unorthodox appearance and ideas were no obstacle to a more than usually rapid promotion. There can be no suggestion of Sartre's revolutionary sympathies stemming from frustrated personal or professional ambition, nor had he any particular financial worries.

A small legacy from his paternal grandmother, combined with their joint salaries, enabled him and Simone de Beauvoir to travel widely in Spain, Greece, France, Germany and even England. In London, they apparently had a serious quarrel when Sartre tried to sum up the essence of the town in a few telling literary and philosophical phrases, while she – perhaps remembering *'La Légende de la Vérité'* – maintained that reality was always greater and more complex than the words used to describe it. Nevertheless, she appreciated the comparison which he made between English cooking and the empiricism of John Locke: both, he maintained, were based on the principle of juxtaposition. *La Force de l'Age* sometimes gives the impression that Sartre and Simone de Beauvoir were less interested in English than in American culture, but they none the less appreciated a writer whom she refers to as Lytton Stracey for the way in which his *Eminent Victorians* 'réduisait à leur vérité certaines grandes figures de salauds' (showed what a few swinishly self-satisfied 'great men' were really like). A more surprising anecdote, for the sensitive English ear, tells what happened after she and Sartre had gone to see Kay Francis in a film entitled *Cynara*. They proceeded to adopt Ernest Dowson's line 'I have been faithful to thee Cynara, in my fashion' as a perfect description of their own relationship.[20]

Before taking the *agrégation*, Sartre had written a *diplôme d'études supérieures* (a kind of MA thesis) on the imagination, and he was asked by Alcan, a publishing house specializing in books on philosophical subjects, if he would like to write a short study of the way in which philosophers had treated this topic. By this

time Sartre had already come into contact with the ideas of
Edmund Husserl and was completing his year in Berlin. According
to Raymond Aron, *L'Etre et le Néant* itself was originally
conceived as a thesis for the *Doctorat d'Etat*,[21] and it would seem
that Sartre might have been aiming at a career as a University
teacher in philosophy. Certainly *L'Imagination*, published in
1936, has all the marks of a thorough, even slightly pedantic
piece of academic research, and its principal interest for the
ordinary, non-philosophical reader of Sartre's work lies almost
exclusively in its last few pages, in the chapter entitled *La
Phénoménologie de Husserl.*

In it, Sartre maintains that it is quite wrong to think of images as
things which we hold before our minds as a man giving a lecture
on painting might put slides into a projector. For instance, if
I imagine my friend Peter's face, I am not examining a kind of
weakened perception, a 'furrow left in consciousness', a faded
snapshot left in my mind from the last time I saw him. I am
making myself conscious of him in a particular way, and doing
something quite different from what I do when I look at him.
Then, I can examine him as he actually is, counting the hairs on
his head if need be. This is something which I can never do when
I imagine he is with me, for there is nothing at all in the image
but what I myself have put there from my memory of what he is
like. It is, as Alain and other philosophers have pointed out,
quite impossible to count the columns on the Parthenon if I call
it to mind only through my imagination. I may know, intellectually,
that it has eight columns on its front because I remember
counting them last time I was in Athens or have read about them
in a book. But this piece of information is something which I
use when I call the image of the building into my mind, not
something which I derive from the image itself. Although
Sartre does not make this point, the actual phrase 'calling to
mind' is one of the ways in which language does express what
happens when we imagine; and there is an interesting similarity
between his ideas and the approach to philosophical problems in
Wittgenstein's *Philosophical Investigations*.

The aim of philosophy, for Wittgenstein, was 'to shew the
fly the way out of the fly-bottle', and one of the central ambitions
of the *Philosophical Investigations* is to make people aware of the
intellectual drawbacks involved in thinking that all games, or
all languages or all mental operations, conform to the same
basic pattern. Similarly, at the beginning of *L'Imagination*, Sartre
talks about the 'mental struggle which must be waged . . . in order
to free ourselves from the almost unshakeable habit of conceiving
all modes of existence as physical in type';[22] and Gilbert Ryle's
observation in *The Concept of Mind* that 'there are no such
objects as mental pictures, and if there were such objects, seeing

them would not be the same as seeming to see faces or mountains' has considerable similarities with Sartre's criticism of how philosophers have gone wrong in the past.[23] In *L'Imagination*, Sartre argues that as long as images were conceived of as things existing in the mind, shuffled about like snapshots at a family reunion, it was impossible to describe them accurately. Only when people recognized that images were 'types of consciousness', mental acts whereby we brought something to mind when it was not there physically, could they be accurately described.

It is this desire to provide an accurate account of how the mind works which informs all Sartre's early published philosophical writing, up to and including *L'Etre et le Néant*. His discovery of Husserl's phenomenology provided him with an invaluable method, but he was by no means an uncritical disciple. His first genuinely philosophical work, the *Essai sur la Transcendance de l'Ego*, published in *Recherches Philosophiques* in 1936,[24] was a fairly vigorous criticism of some of Husserl's more recent views, and especially his postulation of a 'Transcendental Self' as the 'structure of absolute consciousness'. The mind is not, Sartre argues, like a container filled with a mixture of perceptions, emotions, images, hopes, ambitions and fears as a bran tub is filled with jokes, surprises, books and presents. It is a force which projects itself on to the objects of this world, bringing both them and itself into being by its very acts of awareness. And, he maintains in *La Transcendance de l'Ego*, it can do this only if it is not weighed down with a 'transcendent self' that it has to drag along with it in every move.

Sartre's argument here can perhaps be made clearer if we remember the scene in Ibsen's play where Peer Gynt tries to find the essence of the onion. By stripping off its successive skins until there is nothing left, he illustrates the view that there are certain entities which do indeed consist solely of the sum of their parts and nothing more. The picture of the human mind which Sartre puts forward in *La Transcendance de l'Ego* is very similar. If we were to take away the things we see and the thoughts we have, our sufferings, hopes and fears, there would be nothing left, no central Me at all. What keeps us in existence is an 'impersonal spontaneity', and 'unwearying creation of existence of which *we* are not the creators'. To think that we have a central core which always organizes our perceptions and experiences around us as a magnet organizes the iron filings scattered on a piece of paper is an illusion.

In *L'Imaginaire,* the much longer and more ambitious study of the imagination which he published in 1940, Sartre elaborated on the views he had expressed in *L'Imagination* in 1936. There is, he repeats, an essential difference between images and perceptions: the latter are inexhaustible and can always teach us something;

the former are characterized by an 'essential poverty' which
stems from the fact that it is we ourselves who make them up and
can therefore never be surprised by what they contain. Nevertheless, since all acts of consciousness are intentional, images do
have something in common with perceptions. When I look at a
photograph, which is both a real object and a device used for
summoning up images, I do not see merely a collection of black
and white shapes on a piece of thin cardboard. I make sense of
these shapes by projecting on to them what, in some way, I know
they represent: a scene in a garden, a landscape, a girl sitting in
a room. The idea that perception is itself intentional can be
illustrated quite easily by what Sartre does not refer to as
Wittgenstein's duck-rabbit, but which will be most familiar to
English readers in that form:

What distinguishes images from perceptions is not the fact
that we consciously organize the first and are wholly passive
towards the second. The mind is equally active in both cases.
The difference lies in the fact that the objects which we imagine –
paradoxically – not there at the very moment when they are there.
Thus, the face which I conjure up *is* there. I am not lying to
myself when I say that I see Peter in my mind's eye – not in the
way I would be lying if I told somebody that I was thinking of
the Eiffel tower when I was really imagining what he looked like
in a bowler hat. But Peter is nevertheless not there in the room
with me, and it is even a prior condition of my being able to
imagine him that he should not be there. There must therefore,
says Sartre, explaining what he calls the 'Kantian perspectives'[25]
of his method, be some important quality in the human mind
which enables it to postulate, simultaneously, that certain things
both are and are not there. This quality is the power to negate,
the ability effectively to deny its surroundings and summon up a
state of affairs which it knows to be unreal. And, continues
Sartre, the mind can envisage what is not the case only if it is
not wholly absorbed in the reality surrounding it. For the mind
to be able to think in images, it must be able to detach itself
from its present situation. A mind which could not imagine
would be totally *'engluée dans l'existant'* (glued down to what

exists). But since we all can in fact imagine, then we must, in a very important sense of the word, be free. Our mind is not *enlisée* (sucked down by quicksand) or *embourbée* (bogged down) in reality. If it were, then we should always be confronted solely by what is and by nothing more. But since we can summon up, by our imagination, things which are not there at all, then we must be free.

The link between Sartre's attempt to define the imagination and the views which he subsequently puts forward in *L'Etre et le Néant* is most obvious in this insistence upon liberty as a prior condition for the specifically human activity of imagining. The very terms which he uses in *L'Imaginaire* – *enlisée, embourbée, engluée* – are fundamental to the relationship which he describes in *L'Etre et le Néant* between men and things, and to his views on what he calls the 'ontological significance' of stickiness.[26] The importance of *L'Imaginaire* in the development of Sartre's later thinking about literature and society can also be seen by comparing his analysis of what happens when we look at photographs with the argument about reading which forms the basis for the views expressed in *Qu'est-ce que la Littérature?* in 1947. In *L'Imaginaire,* he describes how we animate the photograph by looking at it and using our imagination to bring it to life. In *Qu'est-ce que la Littérature?,* he argues that we do something very similar when we transform what would otherwise be an inert series of little black marks printed on white paper into Raskolnikov's adventures in *Crime and Punishment*. In both cases, we can act as we do only if we are free to see the black and white shapes or the printed characters for what, in any straightforward realistic sense, they are not. A mind which existed solely on the plane of reality, crawling along like a snail on concrete, could never transcend the typographical characters in a novel in such a way as to make them tell a story; and the Sartre of *Qu'est-ce que la Littérature?* carries this argument a stage further by introducing political considerations into what might otherwise remain a piece of neo-Kantian analysis of the conditions necessary to any act of literary understanding. Only in a society where men are politically free, he argues, can the mentally free activity of reading and imagining take on its full significance and develop its full potentialities.

In its immediate biographical context, however, the interest of *L'Imaginaire* is less in the way it prepares the ground for some of Sartre's later political ideas than in its relationship to his childhood. Sartre is far from denying the importance of the imagination, and describes it at one point as 'one of the four or five great functions of the mind'. Yet though it is 'an essential dimension of the mind',[27] the imagination also offers a type of existence which Sartre describes in what often reads like a tone of strong moral disapproval. People can, he says, be divided into two major categories: those who live in the real world; and those who prefer the life of the imagination. It is through a definite choice that people come to live on one mode rather than the other. Even the schizophrenic, in his view, makes a deliberate attempt to avoid the reality principle, and is only an extreme example of a general human tendency sometimes to select an impoverished and unsatisfactory mode of being precisely because of the fewer challenges which it offers.[28] By its very nature, the imaginary world offers neither consistency nor resistance, and he describes the act whereby we imagine something as essentially 'magical', characterized by 'imperious and childlike' qualities, and by 'a refusal to take distance and difficulties into account'.[29] This criticism of the imaginary world is, of course, thoroughly consistent with Sartre's general analysis of what the imagination involves. Since it is possible only by virtue of man's ability to envisage what is not the case, the imagination will by very definition summon up only unreal objects. And since it is by a free choice that we call up imaginary objects, it is only natural that these should be malleable and wholly under our control. What is curious is the similarity between Sartre's evident disapproval, in *L'Imaginaire*, of people who choose imagination rather than reality, and the picture evoked in *Les Mots* of the little boy who consoled himself for his failure to make an impact on the real world of his fellows by seeking refuge in an imaginary universe in which the puny outcast of the Luxembourg gardens could kill a hundred soldiers by a stroke of his pen.

If Sartre does, in *L'Imaginaire*, occasionally slip from the tone of moral neutrality normally expected of a philosopher treating a fairly technical problem of descriptive psychology, his attitude towards the emotions reflects an even more determined attempt to exalt the adult world of reality over the richer emotional life traditionally associated with the child. *Esquisse d'une Théorie des Emotions*, published in 1939, applies to the emotions a method of analysis which is officially the same as the one applied to the imagination in *L'Imaginaire*, and comes up with fairly similar conclusions: emotions are not things which overwhelm us by their own strength; on the contrary, it is we who choose to feel emotions when the real world becomes too difficult for us and we wish to simplify it through magic. In 1946, Sartre was to use this theory of the emotions as the starting point for his analysis of anti-semitism, and the cult of irrationalism characteristic of pre-war fascism in both France and Germany already gave the *Esquisse d'une Théorie des Emotions* a number of political overtones in 1939. It is, however, a less impressive piece of work than either of Sartre's two books on the imagination, and reveals an aspect of his intellectual personality on which Simone de Beauvoir comments several times. Sartre, she remarks, preferred to think in terms of solutions rather than problems, and consequently tended, in discussion, to lay himself open to the more critical and analytical approach adopted at the time by Raymond Aron.[30] There is naturally something attractive in Sartre's attempt to show not only that man ought to control his life by reason but that he can do so if he wishes, and it comes as no surprise to learn, in this context, that he once expressed a strong preference for Corneille over Racine.[31] He may also be quite right to say that the world would be a better place if people did not fool themselves into thinking that their emotions were uncontrollable forces, and tried instead to solve social problems rationally instead of getting angry with certain racial groups. But this does not necessarily make his analysis of emotion as a tool whereby the mind 'degrades itself', and tries to 'take hold in another manner of what it cannot initially bear, by putting itself to sleep, by moving closer to the way it behaves in sleep or hysteria',[32] a convincing account of this particular psycho-physiological phenomenon. Like his view that people freely choose a particular life style when they are about eight years old, the *Esquisse d'une Théorie des Emotions* is an interesting and challenging way of looking at everyday experience. But again like his theory of existential psychoanalysis, it suffers from a serious disadvantage: it would be impossible to devise any experiment which neither confirmed or falsified Sartre's various hypotheses.

L'Imaginaire is less vulnerable to this type of criticism since it is more analytical in its approach. Since his main concern is to infer, from certain agreed properties of the image, which conditions must be fulfilled to make the act of imagining possible, Sartre is not poaching to quite the same extent on the scientist's ground. Nevertheless, his account of the imagination is not totally acceptable. In the last pages of the book he writes about 'the nauseating sickness which characterizes our consciousness of reality',[33] and of the disappointment which we feel on leaving the coherent but unreal world of Beethoven's Seventh Symphony for the humdrum world of everyday life. It is surely fair comment to say that Sartre has got his reader somewhat unfairly into a cleft stick. There appears to be only a Hobson's choice between the satisfactory but evanescent world of the imagination, and the solid but unpleasant world of real life. And if Sartre is still implicitly appealing here to what everybody knows by introspection to be true, there are plenty of people to say that they don't feel at all sickened by the real world. However valid it may be on philosophical grounds, such a reaction nevertheless tends to miss the point as far as Sartre's literary work is concerned.

What matters is the use which he makes of his various obsessions in order to create his own autonomous world, one in which the debate between imagination and reality, begun in his childhood and transposed into philosophical terms in *L'Imaginaire,* is progressively left behind as he concentrates on more far-reaching social, political and ethical questions.

3 'La Nausée', five short stories and literary criticism

i

It was with the publication of *La Nausée*, in June 1938, that Sartre's public literary career really began. The book was immediately successful, and the fact that critics mentioned the names of Kafka, Nietzsche and Proust, when reviewing it in 1938 and 1939, indicates the level of literary and philosophical achievement at which this first novel was immediately placed.[1] Some twenty-five years after deciding to devote his life to writing books, Sartre had achieved at least part of his ambition: that of being recognized by other people as a major writer. It is consequently no surprise to find *La Nausée* mentioned in *Les Mots*, though disappointing that Sartre should have no other detailed comments to make in his autobiography about any of his other novels. 'I brought off, at thirty, this stroke of genius: describing – in all sincerity, I assure you – the unjustified, brackish existence of my fellow-creatures', is how he sums up his achievement, and the very adjectives which he uses evoke the whole atmosphere of his first novel. Yet he is far from showing any pride in his achievement, and immediately insists on how little right he had to use Roquentin as an example while putting himself in the privileged position of the writer who stands above his subject-matter.

It is curious, in this respect, how Sartre's attitude to his novel changes with the passage of years. In 1963, he remarks that it was *bien sincèrement*' that he used Roquentin's fictional experience to describe his own attitude towards the world, and the frequency with which terms of sickness and disgust recur even in his fairly abstract philosophical works seems to indicate that, in the late 1930s and early 1940s at any rate, Roquentin's nausea was his own. The *écoeurement nauséeux* of the closing pages of *L'Imaginaire* recurs as a fundamental aspect of man's experience of the world in *L'Etre et le Néant*, when Sartre talks about the 'dull and inescapable feeling of sickness' which 'perpetually reveals my body to my consciousness'[2], and almost all the characters in *Les Chemins de la Liberté* either feel sick or are sick at some point or other in the story. Roquentin describes both himself and the world as being *de trop*, and the image of sickness and the idea of superfluity are so intimately linked together that it is impossible to say which comes first. This is particularly interesting from a biographical point of view, for it could be argued with equal cogency that Sartre felt as he did because he

had been forcibly struck by the idea that the world had no
creator and consequently no reason to exist at all; or, alternatively,
that he experienced the world as a heaving mass of voluminous
over-abundance, and developed a philosophical theory about the
absence of God and the absurdity of existence because this
made sense of the way he felt. Either way of looking at the novel
would fit in with his remark in *Les Mots* about *l'existence
injustifiée et saumâtre de mes congénères*, for the phrase does
have, as if by accident, one abstract and one physical adjective.
The impression left by the novel is that it is as much a polemical
work as an attempt to use fiction for communicating philosophical
concepts, for when Orestes, the hero of *Les Mouches,* agrees with
Jupiter that his aim is to show men 'their obscene and tasteless
existence, which is given to them for no purpose',[3] he is expressing
Sartre's own ideas and personal experience just as clearly and
forcibly as Roquentin and seems almost as keen to bring other
people round to his way of thinking.

In May 1954, however, Sartre gave a very different impression
of how his own experience could be linked with that of
Roquentin. He declared, in an interview published in the review
Club, that he personally had never had an attack of nausea,
which was 'a fictional way of expressing something vague'. The
implication is that he had been using the idea of physical sickness
simply as a kind of rhetorical device, but it is difficult to reconcile
this with the remark in *L'Etre et le Néant* that The Other 'perpetually
lives his facticity in nausea as a non-positional apprehension of a
contingency that he is'.[4] This sentence surely means that everyone
really feels as sick as Roquentin, though without always realizing
it, and this coincidence between Roquentin's experience and
one of the major themes in *L'Etre et le Néant* would fit in with
Sartre's obvious intention to use his novels and plays as means of
persuading his readers to adopt new ways of thinking and feeling.
The Sartre who made Mathieu Delarue, in *L'Age de Raison*,
describe existence as 'drinking oneself without being thirsty',
cannot be merely playing with words when he depicts
Antoine Roquentin as 'veule, alangui, obscène, digérant,
ballottant de mornes pensées' (flabby, drooping, obscene,
digesting, shuffling my miserable ideas),[5] and he is well within
the traditions established by his Alsatian Protestant forbears in
thus using literature for highly personal didactic ends.

Sartre's analysis and dismissal of his literary career in *Les Mots*
significantly omits an essential factor which the immediate
success and continued appeal of *La Nausée* brings out very well:
he is a good writer and he has something to say. At several
times in *Les Mots*, one is reminded of the famous *Punch* cartoon
about the young man who had just come down from the University
and announced his intention of becoming a Writer. 'But what are

you going to write about?', his aunt asks him. 'My dear Aunt', he replies in tones of utmost disdain, 'one doesn't write *about* anything; one just Writes'. The joke is not without relevance to the ideals proposed by the French 'New Novelists' of the 1950s and the aims followed by the team of *Tel Quel*, but it is in no way appropriate to any of Sartre's books. Whether he was trying to free himself from certain physical obsessions by describing them in a book, or whether he was cleverly finding a physical equivalent for a particular idea, he was not 'just Writing'. He was using language to express an acute and original world vision, and one which matched the brooding, disillusioned atmosphere of the times. W. H. Auden's remark about the artist being the 'antenna of the race' is peculiarly appropriate to all the fiction which Sartre published before the outbreak of the World War II, and the Bouville of *La Nausée* is, for all its solid, nineteenth-century buildings, not unlike the Slough on which John Betjeman wished the bombs to fall. What is also especially interesting is the way Sartre expresses the imminent collapse of a civilization without ever falling into a purely private vision, and without moving so far from the traditional function of the novel that his work loses all appeal to the ordinary reader.

It is, indeed, remarkable how many of the established criteria of the novel are applicable to *La Nausée*. It tells a story, describes a social and geographical *milieu*, presents three major characters and an interesting sprinkling of minor ones, criticizes the present structure and past history of a particular society, and contains within itself both a would-be novelist and a meditation on the art of the novel. It is also, in parts, a very funny book, as well as a compelling presentation, in fictional terms, of several important philosophical ideas. On an aesthetic plane, as George Bauer has recently shown, it can be convincingly interpreted as a transposition of the themes in Dürer's *Melencolia*, and it is significant that *Melancholia* was the title which Sartre had originally intended to give it.[6] It is also the only work by Sartre to present an aesthetic solution as a possibly valid response to the problem of the world's absurdity, and which might therefore be seriously considered as the prolongation of the attitude described in *Les Mots*. Nevertheless, a number of other features of the novel show that Sartre was by no means the uncritical supporter of the social *status quo* that he describes himself as being in his autobiography, and there are many other aspects of *La Nausée* which distinguish it sharply from the kind of book held up for Sartre's admiration by his grandfather.

La Nausée tells a fairly clear story of how a problem makes itself felt, how it is solved, and how some important philosophical and literary discoveries are made. At the beginning of the novel, Antoine Roquentin is puzzled because physical objects seem to be undergoing a change. He is so affected by a flat pebble which he picks up to play ducks and drakes that he throws it away in disgust. His beer glass seems odd and inexplicable; and he cannot bring himself to pick up a piece of paper that he sees lying on the pavement in front of him. As the novel progresses, he gradually comes to understand why the stone gave him a kind of 'nausée dans les mains', and why a fork in a restaurant seems to take on an independent life of its own. It is because nothing in the world of natural objects carries its own definition within itself, because there is a contingency about the whole universe, an absurdity which can never be remedied. A circle, he explains, is neither contingent nor absurd. It does carry its own definition within itself, being defined, with no references to natural objects, as the rotation of a straight line about one of its extremities. He finds the key to 'Existence, to his attacks of nausea, to his own life' when he realizes that this logical, mathematical necessity does not extend to the world of objects, when he understands that 'Every existing thing is born for no reason, carries on living through weakness, and dies by accident'.[7] And if there is no final means of overcoming this absurdity, at least Roquentin has understood why he personally has had the experience of nausea which dominates the novel.

When the novel begins, Roquentin is writing a book on the life of an eighteenth-century adventurer, Monsieur de Rollebon. However, as he discovers that there is no form or shape in his own existence, he realizes how false it is to try to reconstruct the events of somebody else's life in an orderly and significant manner, and gives up trying to write his book. He is not in any way financially dependent on his work, since a small legacy provides him with just enough to live on – perhaps the way Sartre looked upon his salary as a schoolteacher – and his needs are very modest. His aim in writing about Monsieur de Rollebon had been to create a kind of art form out of real events. Once he is forced to recognize that it is he and he alone who must freely decide what meaning these events shall have, he can no longer use M. de Rollebon's life as a way of justifying his own. The only way in which he can think of giving some kind of shape to his existence is by writing a completely different kind of book, one which resembles a piece of music or a mathematical proposition in that it carries its own definition within itself. At several points in the novel, Roquentin finds temporary relief from his nausea by listening to an old recording of *Some of These Days*, and this jazz tune plays the same role in the argument of *La Nausée* as Beethoven's Seventh Symphony does in the closing pages of *L'Imaginaire*. In both cases, the work of art represents an internally consistent world that does not depend upon physical existence. Even if he were to break the record, thinks Roquentin, it would

make no difference to the tune. Because this does not depend
upon things that merely exist – the wax of the actual record, the
needle, the café in which it is played – it belongs to a different
realm. It *is*. And the book which Roquentin hopes eventually to
write will have something of this same quality. It will not, unlike
his projected work on Monsieur de Rollebon, depend upon
material objects which have all at some time or other been
tainted with the unavoidable contingency of existing things.
It will, as far as we can gather, be a work of pure form, in which
one element follows another with the inevitability of the steps
in a piece of mathematical reasoning or the notes in a piece of
music. The novel ends with Roquentin's decision to commit
himself to the writing of this book, and with an image of puri-
fication:'Tomorrow, it will rain on Bouville'. He has understood his
problem and found what he thinks may be a valid way of dealing
with it.

Although this aesthetic solution does seem consistent with
some of the ideas in *Les Mots*, the rest of *La Nausée* makes
it very different from the kind of book that Charles Schweitzer
would have liked his grandson to write. To begin with, it is
extremely disrespectful towards established society. At one point,
Roquentin visits the municipal art gallery at Bouville. He surveys
the portraits of the local worthies who, in the nineteenth century,
raised Bouville to the status of the third port in France. After
enumerating all their faults, from their physical weaknesses to
their political ruthlessness and lack of moral scruples, he ends
by addressing them as 'Swine' (*Salauds*). It is equally consistent
with Roquentin's instinctive sympathy with the outcasts of
bourgeois society that he should describe *Some of These Days*,
the jazz tune which inspires him with the idea of writing his own
book, as having been composed by a Jew and sung by a Negress,
and this clearly anticipates Sartre's own support, later in his
career, for the victims of a racialist attitude which he regards
as peculiar to the middle class. In the context of Roquentin's
visit to the portrait gallery, however, as well as in that of Sartre's
later essay *Matérialisme et Révolution*, the Jew and the Negress
also have other qualities that make them particularly attractive to
Roquentin. Even those local worthies who might appear, by normal
standards, to have lived good and noble lives are still regarded by
both Roquentin and Sartre himself as fundamentally dishonest.
They are all convinced that they have the right to exist, and have
even paid a number of commercially successful artists to depict
them in such a way as to eliminate all traces of the vagueness
and injustifiability of life as it actually is. Their great crime is
less what they did than how they thought of themselves: men of
divine right, Lords of Creation, when Roquentin's own intuition
has told him that no living thing whatsoever had any reason at

all even to be alive. This is something which, according to Sartre, Jews, Negresses and members of the oppressed working classes also realize instinctively, and the semi-philosophical basis for his later socialism is here quite visible in his first novel.

Charles Schweitzer's own attitude towards society was one of intense respect, mingled with the certainty that the evil represented in the past by the machinations of Kings and Emperors had been finally vanquished by the triumph of the 'Republican Principles' of 1789. Sartre and Roquentin are less confident. Under the calm appearance of the sea lies a crawling mass of sinister beasts, and the very existence of crabs and shellfish bears witness to the mystery, unpredictability and total strangeness of the animal world. Beneath the apparent calm of the European society which Bouville reflects in its most stable form, the forces of evil which were to lead, in September 1939, to the outbreak of the World War II, had already begun to make their presence felt. In 1933, Hitler had come to power in Germany, and established a régime which, by 1938, was clearly aiming to conquer Europe. Although there is no mention in *La Nausée* of any political event later than 1920, the middle class is clearly about to be engulfed in the six years of war which began only a year after Sartre's first novel was published. Moreover, man's position in the world described in *La Nausée* is one that dooms him to unhappiness even under the most perfect of political régimes. According to *L'Etre et le Néant*, he is condemned perpetually to strive to transcend his situation as a conscious being aware of its own contingency, but is perpetually unable to attain the only status which will really enable him to fulfil this ambition: that of a being which is because it is, *ens causa sui*, God. Roquentin's nausea takes him to the first stage of Sartre's argument, and gives him an intuition of what it is like to be fully conscious of what Sartre calls, on the last page of *L'Etre et le Néant*, the 'useless passion' of mankind.[8] Peculiar though Roquentin's experience may at first sight appear, the discovery which he makes about his contingency is a statement of the obvious. Matters of fact are not logically necessary, since by very definition the bus cannot leave the station at eight o'clock with the same inevitability and necessity that the next prime number after three is five. If the inhabitants of Bouville feel reassured at living in a regular universe where 'bodies in a vacuum all fall at the same speed, the public garden is closed everyday at four o'clock in winter and at six in summer, lead melts at 338 degrees centigrade, the last tram leaves the Town Hall at five minutes past eleven',[9] then they have made the mistake of confusing regularity with inevitability. David Hume would certainly have regarded this aspect of Roquentin's argument as reflecting his own view that 'necessity is something that exists in the mind, not in objects',[10] as well as consistent with his rejection of causal connection in favour of constant conjunction. Once one thinks about it, it is difficult to disagree with Sartre's contention that, in the absence of God, there is no reason for things to be as they are and no guarantee that they will not suddenly change. To have put this idea into fictional terms was itself a major achievement, and Sartre's lack of enthusiasm for *La Nausée* is yet one more puzzling feature of *Les Mots*.

ii

One year after the appearance of *La Nausée*, in July 1939, Sartre published his second work of imaginative fiction: a volume of five short stories entitled *Le Mur*. In certain circles in English-speaking countries, this volume is still perhaps his best-known work. It was the first to appear in paper-back form, under the appetizing title of *Intimacy*, and with the following quotation from *Punch* on its rather lurid cover: 'Leaves *Lady Chatterley's Lover* standing at the post.'[11] Like Lawrence's novel, however, it is a fundamentally serious work. Each of the stories deals with a particular physical or emotional experience, and does so with the intention of illustrating a definite philosophical point. In the first, *Le Mur*, the story which gives its title to the collection, Sartre is concerned to refute Heidegger's contention that man can live meaningfully towards his own death. In the second, *La Chambre*, he continues his investigation into the relationship between imagination and reality, and makes his first attempt to treat the theme of sequestration. The third, *Intimité*, deals with the concept of *mauvaise foi* (bad faith), the major ruse which we adopt in order to avoid recognizing that we are free. The fourth, *Erostrate*, is an exploration of the nature of sadism, and perhaps a satirical extension of the extreme 'anti-humanism' adopted by Roquentin. The fifth, *L'Enfance d'un Chef*, is the most obviously political of all the texts that Sartre published before World War II: a study of how anti-semitism makes a particular appeal to those members of the *bourgeoisie* who cannot stand up to the idea of their own liberty and contingency. In all the stories, however, the same puritan distrust of the body, coupled in two of them with a neo-Protestant insistence on the need to stick to the decisions reached according to a privately recognized inner light, gives Sartre's atheist exploration of the human condition some very odd overtones.

Throughout the first volume of *Les Chemins de la Liberté*, *L'Age de Raison*, Mathieu Delarue is haunted by feelings of guilt and regret that he did not follow the example of his friend Gomez and join up on the side of the legally constituted Spanish republican government when Franco organized his military

rising in March 1936. The opening story, *Le Mur,* indicates
that Sartre himself was not held back by any doubts as to which
side was in the right, and it could be read, like some of the
Hemingway short stories which it so much resembles, as a
statement of political sympathy. Yet while it is certainly an
implicit denunciation of right-wing brutality and injustice –
one of the republicans about to be shot by Franco's supporters
has never been politically active – this is not its main purpose.
Sartre's analysis is concentrated on the feelings which Pablo
Ibbieta has towards his own death, and the effort which he
makes to give some meaning to it by one final action. For
Heidegger, the thinker with whom Sartre seems to be concerned
in this story,[12] dying is an act which no other person can do
for one. It is also something which men can transform from a
passively experienced fatality into an actively experienced and
apprehended destiny. By living towards his own death man can
give it meaning, as Kyo Gisors, in Malraux's *La Condition
Humaine,* makes his death into the crowning moment of his life
by killing himself while a political prisoner in the hands of the
Kuomintang. For Sartre, however, this is not possible, and the
anecdote which provides the basis for *Le Mur* illustrates this
idea with rather suspicious neatness.

Pablo Ibbieta is led, by his discovery that nothing has any
meaning once death is seen as immediate and inevitable, to play
a joke on his captors. They are prepared to release him if he will
tell them where one of his friends, Ramon Gris, is hiding.
Pablo knows, but has no intention of telling the fascists. Instead,
he decides to send them on a wild-goose chase by saying that
Gris is hiding in the cemetery. Since nothing matters, he might as
well have a good laugh. But the world is so absurd that nothing
can be relied upon. A few days previously, Ramon had left his
safe hiding place with his cousin, and gone to the cemetery.
Pablo's desire to use his own death to have the last laugh turns
completely against him. When he learns from another prisoner
that Ramon has been shot while resisting arrest, he collapses in
hysterics.

The second of these short stories, *La Chambre,* takes the reader
completely away from the hard, physical world of Pablo and
his companions. Instead, we are in the claustrophobic world of the
French bourgeoisie which Sartre knew so well. At one point in
La Force de l'Age, Simone de Beauvoir seems to suggest that
Madame Lemaire, whose husband refused to leave his room,
provided the starting point for *La Chambre.*[13] However, it is
equally possible that Sartre's early experience as a sequestered
child is relevant to the frequency with which this theme recurs in
his work, and perhaps significant that the motives for which Eve,
whose husband is going mad, keeps him in his room are those of

a devoted but possessive love. *La Chambre* was first published in review form in January 1938, and is in many respects closer to the preoccupations of *L'Imaginaire* than to the aims of *La Nausée*. Its superiority to the other stories in the volume is partly explicable by Sartre's restraint in not making it into a straight-forward case history illustrating some of the views about schizophrenia expressed in *L'Imaginaire*. He must have been tempted to follow out the implications of his own remark that the schizophrenic 'knows perfectly well that the objects with which he surrounds himself are unreal: it is for that very reason that he makes them appear',[14] and at one point Eve suspects that her husband does not really believe in the flying statues which invade the room and persecute him. However, the actual events of the story imply a much greater recognition that the human mind is not quite so firmly in control of itself as some of the passages in *L'Imaginaire* would seem to suggest, and it is significant in this respect that our attention should be concentrated throughout on Eve, who is not mad, rather than on Pierre, who is. Eve's love for her husband is so great that she would like to join him in the magical but terrifying world into which he is plunged when the statues fly around him. Yet at the very moment when she is on the point of believing that this is about to happen, she hears a noise in the corridor outside. Immediately, she recognizes it as her servant Marie, and remembers that she must pay her for the gas. No one can go mad voluntarily, and the wall which gives its title to the whole collection takes on an obviously symbolic meaning when Pierre tells Eve: 'Il y a un mur entre toi et moi. Je te vois, je te parle, mais tu es de l'autre côté.' What is more important, however, is Sartre's recognition, both through his description of how Eve behaves and in his more ambiguous account of Pierre, that the human mind is not the wholly free and totally conscious force described in *L'Imaginaire* and the *Esquisse d'une théorie des émotions*. There seems to be no reason to question the diagnosis attributed in the story to the psychiatrist Franchot, according to which Pierre is in the grip of a disease which will reduce him, within three years, to a purely animal level.

Just as it is quite clear, in *Le Mur*, that Sartre is on the side of Pablo Ibbieta and his friends, and against the fascists, so it is equally obvious, in *La Chambre*, that he infinitely prefers Pierre and Eve to Monsieur and Madame Darbédat, Eve's parents. Monsieur Darbédat, in particular, decreeing that Pierre should be packed off 'in his own best interest' to a home where he will be happy with people of his own kind, is an example of bourgeois self-satisfaction at its worst. Far better, Sartre suggests, either to be mad or try desperately to sympathize with the mad, than adapt oneself to a world run by people like this. The existentialist

preference for the eccentric over the abnormal is at its most
challenging in this story, and perhaps more effective through being
suggested rather than explicitly stated. From a rational point of
view, Monsieur Darbédat is probably right, and he has medical
opinion behind him. But as far as understanding the human
condition is concerned, he doesn't even get to first base. Those
who, like Pablo Ibbieta, are facing death, or those who are in
what Jaspers would call the 'boundary situation' of grappling
with their own or other people's madness, are in a far better
position to understand what it is like to be a human being.
'Madmen tell the truth', says Johanna in *Les Séquestrés d'Altona*,
when explaining to her rather conventional husband Werner
why she prefers his brilliant but apparently insane brother
Frantz, and adds that: 'There is only one: the horror of
being alive.'[15] This is what knowing Frantz has enabled her to
discover, and Sartre's position in this respect does not change
between 1938 and 1959. Better Socrates dissatisfied than a pig
satisfied, said John Stuart Mill. Better the mad who know than
the respectable citizens who live in the world of illusion, echoes
Sartre.

The third story in the volume, *Erostrate*, differs from the first
two both in the manner of its composition and in the kind of
moral judgments which it suggests. It is told in the form of
an interior monologue, and the style thus exactly fits the
obsessional, solipsistic world of the person it describes. It is the
first example in Sartre's work of a man who fails to do what he
sets out to do because of some weakness within himself, and thus
perhaps his first rather paradoxical venture into ethics. Like the
Garcin of *Huis Clos*, who had staked everything on the idea that
he was a brave man and who runs away at the moment of crisis,
or like Philippe Grésigne, in *Le Sursis*, who sets out to defy
society but ends up by handing himself over to the police,
Paul Hilbert is a man who lives for an idea. This idea is that he
will defy all the good people by a pointless but perfect crime,
just as Hierostratus achieved an immortality denied to its
architect by burning down the temple of Diana at Ephesus. His
crime will be to go down in the street, shoot the first five people
he sees, and then kill himself with the last bullet left in his
revolver; and he writes the same letter to two hundred famous
French humanist writers to tell them exactly what he is going to
do and why.

His plan is similar to André Breton's famous definition of the
simplest surrealist action as going down and firing at random
into the crowd.[16] However, Hilbert fails to achieve any of the
black perfection of his plan. He panics, shoots only one person,
runs away in the wrong direction, and has to hide in the lavatory
of a café. There, instead of shooting himself, he quietly surrenders.

Had he succeeded, one feels that the Sartre who showed such hostility in *La Nausée* to the writers who believed in Man, in the consolations afforded by Art, and in the Beauty and Tragedy of Human Existence, would not have been too unhappy. Hilbert would at least have set out to do what he intended, and the description of his crime as a 'glittering mineral' (*minéral étincelant*) standing in men's path, is reminiscent of the images which Roquentin uses to describe the work of art which he hopes will make men afraid of their existence.

Like a number of other texts which Sartre wrote in the late thirties and early forties, like *Huis Clos* and to some extent like *L'Age de Raison* and *Baudelaire, Erostrate* also offers a negative but not necessarily ironic definition of what later came to be known as the existentialist ethic. Cast in the terms which used to be popular in 1970, this ethic recommends that one should 'do one's thing' and ¦be damned to the consequences. That, at least until Sartre became more ostensibly concerned with social matters, could well be taken as the message both of *Erostrate* and of *L'Age de Raison*. Neither Paul Hilbert nor Mathieu Delarue has the courage of his own convictions. Like Baudelaire, they pretend to rebel against bourgeois society; but they fail, as he does, to take their rebellion through to the end.

A theme that recurs in Sartre's work is the way in which we define other people by looking at them. In *Le Mur* itself, it is only when Pablo feels that the Belgian doctor is looking at him that he realizes how profusely he is sweating, while in *La Chambre* Eve detests the way in which her father, having looked at Pierre, can carry away this image of their life together and judge them both. In *L'Etre et le Néant*, Sartre bases much of his analysis of human relationships on the idea that I am always trying to make people look at me in a particular way, while they are always refusing to fall in with my desires and are trying, instead, to make me see them in the way they prefer. One possible avenue of escape from this universe of conflicting glances can be found, according to Sartre, in the sexual and emotional phenomenon of sadism. The sadist, he argues, tries to reduce the other person to a purely passive pair of eyes, one that will see him exactly as he wants to be seen. This ambition, on any long-term basis, is both self-defeating and impossible to maintain. The other person's eyes are worth capturing only in so far as they are the clearest and most visible expression of his freedom, and once captured are consequently no longer worth having. Moreover, no-one can permanently enslave another person's mind, any more than he can give up his own freedom, and the sadist cannot win.[17] Nevertheless, sadism can be a satisfying temporary expedient, and a visit which Hilbert pays to a prostitute during

the period when he is waiting to commit his crime illustrates
with particular clarity how sex can be used in this way. When he
forces the woman to undress and walk about in front of him,
while he himself sits motionless and fully clothed in an armchair,
Hilbert reduces her to a wholly vulnerable and contingent piece
of flesh whose terrified eyes reveal how completely it is under
his control. The description of this scene, which culminates in
an unobtrusive orgasm on Hilbert's part, was selected by a
Monsieur René Varin in 1949 for inclusion in a collection
of texts entitled *L'Erotisme dans la Littérature Française*.[18] It
has a certain compulsive charm, and again shows Sartre writing
a very different type of book to the ones held up for his admiration
by Charles Schweitzer.

It is naturally tempting to say that no general conclusions can
be drawn from the behaviour of so peculiar an individual as Paul
Hilbert. Sartre's insistence on the way people express conflict by
looking at one another might also be attributed to the fact that he
has only one eye, and he has always been rather vulnerable to a
reductionist approach. He has also, in *Les Mots*, provided
hostile critics with a whole battery of arguments against him,
and the atmosphere of his early work does seem to suggest that
he was a little odd. His analysis of human relationships in *L'Etre
et le Néant* can be seen as a development of the way in which an
only child sees the world, as a battlefield of isolated wills, and his
apparent failure even to envisage the possibility, in his literary and
philosophical work, that human life can be enjoyable on an
ordinary level can also be read as an attempt to avenge himself
for his unhappy childhood. The fact remains, however, that all
attempts to reduce Sartre's ideas either to the traumas produced
in him by his extraordinary childhood, or to some other private
experience which he has not so far had the generosity to reveal,
are open to an important objection. Simone de Beauvoir
formulated it most neatly when she told of how she answered the
people who told her that she thought such and such a thing
because she was a woman. 'Not at all', she would reply, 'I think
it because it is true.' And there is one essential aspect of Sartre's
philosophy which is extremely difficult to explain away by his
personal peculiarities: his vision of human freedom.

In the volume entitled *Le Mur*, it is the short story *Intimité*
which expresses Sartre's concept of freedom most clearly and
most convincingly. The anecdote is a simple one: Lulu, a shop-
girl, is married to a dull and apparently impotent man called
Henri. She is being urged by her friend Rirette to run away with
her lover, Pierre, and spends most of the story trying to avoid the
moment when she will have to take a decision. After she has eventually been badgered by Rirette into leaving Henri, she carefully
arranges to be walking along the Boulevard du Montparnasse at

the very moment when Henri is bound to come along and find her. When this happens, it fits in very well with her plan of leaving decisions to other people, and she allows Rirette and Henri to pull her backwards and forwards 'as if she were a bundle of laundry'[19] rather than make up her own mind what to do. In the end, she does go off with Pierre, but accidentally arranges for Henri to find out where she is staying. He comes to fetch her back, and the story ends with Rirette being 'overwhelmed by a bitter regret' at not being able to arrange her friend's life for her.

There are, in fact, two aspects to Sartre's view of human liberty in *L'Intimité*, and it could be argued that they are not both equally convincing. On the one hand, Sartre offers a very perceptive analysis of how one particular person refuses to take a decision, and in this respect his ideas are wholly acceptable. However, he also insists that people are fully in command of their bodies, and this is obviously more open to question. Thus, it is a matter of common experience that we do find a certain relief in having the responsibility for some decisions taken out of our hands, and this relief can in itself be seen as a recognition that we do, basically, look upon ourselves as free. If Lulu wanted to, she could have avoided meeting Henri, abstained from giving him the address of her hotel, and begun a new life with Pierre. It is she who decides that she is a particular kind of person by finally not going away with Pierre. It is not the kind of person she already is which makes her stay with Henri.

One of Sartre's most important ideas, and one which, like so much of his early work, is on the borderline between philosophy and psychology, is that of bad faith (*mauvaise foi*), the intellectual and emotional sleight-of-hand whereby we try to hide our freedom from ourselves. *Intimité* gives a very persuasive account of how this bad faith works in one specific instance, and Sartre's implicit appeal to his reader's own experience is well within the phenomenologist tradition. Just as, in *L'Imagination* and *L'Imagin-aire*, he set out from the idea that everyone spontaneously distinguishes between perceptions and images, so he assumes in *Intimité* that everyone will recognize Lulu's bad faith as fundamentally akin to their own. This is quite acceptable, and the only reservations which one might have about the philosophical implications of *Intimité* come from the second aspect of Sartre's view of human liberty: the one which stems from his rejection of the subconscious, and insistence on man's ability to impose virtually complete control over his emotive behaviour as well as his physical actions. Lulu maintains, throughout the interior monologues in which she explains her reluctance to go away with Pierre, that she is incapable of enjoying normal sexual relations with a man, and can do nothing to alter this since it is 'medical'.[20] It might perhaps seem a little odd, if this is the case, that she should agree to have anything at all to do with Pierre, but this inconsistency is part and parcel of the vision which Sartre has of her character. Her motives also become easier to understand if one remembers his acceptance, in *L'Etre et le Néant*, of Stekel's view that frigidity in women always stems from a conscious choice.[21] She is quite happy to receive the emotional flattery involved in being pursued by an attractive man like Pierre, but refuses to let herself go and pay what Victorian novelists would call the full physical price. A cartoon in the London *Evening Standard* for 26 March 1959 depicted a woman saying to her friend: 'I want to be swept off my feet by somebody I can bend to my will', and Lulu is interesting and acceptable as a fictional character whose actions reflect a widespread tendency. But it is a long way to argue from this that all cases of frigidity are conscious in origin, and that every single one of our acts stems from a conscious choice.

Perhaps one reason why Sartre is more generally admired as a novelist than he is as a philosopher is that his fiction and plays do not necessarily involve, for their appreciation, the acceptance of sweeping statements about the free choice made by the schizophrenic, the conscious origin of complexes, the inevitability of conflict, or the sickness which all human beings should experience when they realize that their life is given to them for no purpose. They can be read as interesting observations on certain types of human behaviour, and it is in some ways a disadvantage that there should be so close and so frequent a correlation between his cautionary tales and his philosophical views. *Intimité*, for example, is an entertaining study of the sexual mores apparently prevalent in lower-middle-class Parisian society in the 1930s. Its style is a delightful example of Sartre's ability to mimic certain speech habits and modes of thought, and it also contains some interesting sociological observations. Like the other characters whose sexual behaviour is described in Sartre's fiction – Mathieu Delarue, Boris Serguine, Mathieu's army friend Pinette – Pierre and Lulu practise *coitus interruptus*.[22] The frequency of this practice is perhaps not irrelevant to the generally rather disillusioned account of sexuality found in Sartre's work, and it certainly offers an interesting clue as to how the French managed to avoid a high birth-rate in a country where contraceptives were, until recently, officially banned. But there is a wide gap between offering what might be called a morally neutral account of Lulu's behaviour in terms of her dishonesty and the effect which the sexual customs of her class have had upon her, and using this as a springboard for a series of moral and philosophical generalizations. A smoking-room story tells how Lloyd George's fiancée told her mother that she was rather nervous about what was going to happen on her wedding night, and received the reply: 'There are some moments in a woman's life when all she can do is grit her teeth and think of England'. The views that Sartre expresses about complexes in *L'Être et le Néant* would not only require Lulu to grit her teeth; she would have to make up her mind to enjoy it if it killed her.

Oddly enough, however, the only person in *Le Mur* who does make a choice is quite obviously satirized for making the wrong one. Lucien Fleurier, in the last and longest story, *L'Enfance d'un Chef*, decides to escape from the uncertainty about his own identity which has haunted him all his life by becoming an anti-semite. His adoption of a fascist ideology is presented by Sartre as being a free action, though one to which Lucien was predisposed by his social class. *L'Enfance d'un Chef* is, in this respect, the most openly political of all Sartre's pre-war writings.

It is also a story in which Sartre tries to criticize not only fascism but also the odd mixture of Freudianism and surrealism which flourished in some French literary circles between the wars. On emerging from childhood into adolescence, Lucien becomes friendly with a classmate called Berliac, who uses the surrealist technique of 'automatic writing' to obtain what seem, from the extracts which Sartre quotes of them, to be extraordin-arily bad poems in the style of Rimbaud or Lautréamont. Later, he almost quarrels with Lucien over whose turn it is to pay for some drinks, and diagnoses what he calls his friend's 'avarice' – in fact, a refusal to stand the fifth successive round – as a sign that Lucien is still in the anal stage and must have been potty-trained too late. The two nevertheless stay friends long enough for Berliac to introduce Lucien to a magnificently bogus surrealist poet called Bergère. There follows an unpleasant homosexual relationship between Lucien and Bergère, until what Sartre ironically presents as the former's basic soundness of character enables him to get back into the ordinary world of bourgeois morality and have an affair with a working-class lady called Maud. With his sex life alternating between some unpleasant real experiences and a more attractive, and as yet Platonic, admiration for Pierrette Guigard, the sister of one of his class-mates, Lucien settles down. He gradually realizes that he can fulfill himself only through an identification with the soil and soul of France. On adopting an attitude of violent hostility to the Jews, those rationalist intruders into the solid universe of the real France, he feels his previous uncertainties melt away. He is invaded by a sense of his own rights, and totally escapes from what he now sees as the illusory view that he existed 'by chance and was merely drifting through life'. He becomes a Leader, one whose right to command will remain undiminished by the obedience of generations of workmen, one who has cast aside 'the intimacy of the mucous membrane . . . the sadness of the flesh, the ignoble lie of equality' in order to become 'an immense bouquet of responsibilities and of rights'.[23] For Lucien, anti-semitism is a means to an end, not an end in itself. And what it provides is an escape from the human condition, his transformation, as Sartre was to put it a few years later in the *Réflexions sur la Question Juive*, from a mere man into a pitiless rock, a raging torrent, a devastating thunder-bolt.[24]

L'Enfance d'un Chef is perhaps the most obvious example, in the whole of Sartre's work, of how he exploits his personal obsessions and philosophical convictions to produce a political conclusion. The correlation between this story and the *Réflexions sur la Question Juive* is so close that it is only the historical references which enable the reader to decide which was written first. A footnote in the *Réflexions* gives the date of composition as October 1944, but the essay could just as easily be read as a commentary on the story as the story could be told as an illustration of the essay. Sartre describes anti-semites in general in terms that are very similar to those which he uses to speak of Lucien, mentioning their 'inconsistance profonde' and arguing that they adopt an attitude of unshakeable hostility towards the Jews because they are attracted by 'la permanence de la pierre'. The anti-semite chooses hatred because this is the way in which he can avoid having to solve problems rationally and escape from 'the overwhelming responsibility of thinking for himself',[25] and it is precisely because Lucien is impatient to arrive at a rapid solution to his problems that he chooses to think of himself as 'pitiless and pure . . . a steel blade threatening other breasts'. The horror for his own physical existence attributed to Lucien by the use of phrases such as 'intimité de muqueuse' is also clearly something, whatever disclaimers he may have made in 1954, which Sartre himself experienced in the 1930s.

Like Sartre's other villains, Lucien is a member of the middle class. In the *Réflexions sur la Question Juive*, Sartre states explicitly that anti-semitism is a middle-class phenomenon, and maintains that it is rarely found either in the proletariat or in those members of the middle class who, like engineers, have to use rational criteria in their day to day work. However much of an indirect tribute the second part of this statement may be towards the atmosphere which Monsieur Mancy made prevail in Sartre's second home, the first part is very vulnerable to purely factual criticisms. It is, nevertheless, consistent with the description which Sartre provides, in *L'Enfance d'un Chef*, of the atmosphere in which Lucien grew up. He was almost as over-protected as Sartre himself, and it is perhaps not surprising if other critics apart from Marc Beigbeder should have interpreted the story in a semi-autobiographical light. In so far as Lucien

has a father and ends up as a fascist, they were clearly wrong to
do so. Nevertheless, the Lucien who plays at being Lucien,
and who is never sure of what he really feels or thinks, is not
unlike the young Jean-Paul who was so infected by his grandfather's histrionics that he could not tell whether he preferred
steak or veal.[26]

The short stories in *Le Mur* are perhaps the best introduction
to Sartre's early work, for they show both his basic philosophical
ideas and his moral and political preferences in their clearest
light. They naturally gain from being seen in the context of his
other books, and it cannot be just coincidence that a girl called
Maud, briefly mentioned in *Le Sursis*, should have had an affair,
before the action of the novel takes place, with someone called
Lucien who turned out to be a coward.[27] The politically committed
Sartre of the 1940s is already there in *L'Enfance d'un Chef*,
just as the earlier Sartre, with his interest in the problems of the
imagination, is there in *La Chambre*. All he needed to do, when
his experience as a prisoner of war and member of the resistance
showed him the need for the writer to concern himself with
political matters, was transform his criticism of the middle
class into a more active attempt to change the structure of the
society in which he lived. Moreover, the general world view that
emerges from both *La Nausée* and *Le Mur* needed only a
sharper and more dramatic definition to become the challenging
body of philosophical and ethical doctrines which became known,
immediately after the liberation of France in 1944, as Sartrean
existentialism. Man is free, but his discovery of this freedom is
not a particularly exhilarating or joyous experience. He is cast
into a world in which he has no preordained or privileged
position, and feels anguish at the realization that he and he alone
must invent the values by which he can live. Under the impact
of war, defeat and occupation, Sartre was led to develop these
ideas in such a way as to make them into an extraordinarily
accurate description of what it was like to be alive in mid-twentieth-
century Europe. He may, in doing so, have written books which
were the opposite of what he wanted, and betrayed the ambitions
fostered by Charles Schweitzer's selfishness. But he produced
some remarkably fine work, and the ten years between the
publication of *La Nausée* in June 1938 and the first performance
of *Les Mains Sales* in April 1948 constitute what is, up to now,
the highwater mark of his literary career.

iii

The success which Sartre enjoyed in literary circles before the
outbreak of World War II was not confined to his own novels
and short stories. He also made a name for himself as a literary

critic and visibly imposed his mark on each and every author he discussed. In particular, he used Mauriac, Dos Passos, Faulkner or Camus as examples to illustrate what he thought the novel should be like if it is to reflect man's true relationship with the social and physical world which he inhabits. First of all comes the way the story is told. 'A technique of narration always involves a novelist's metaphysic. The critic's task is to elucidate the latter before appreciating the former', he declares when discussing Faulkner's *The Sound and the Fury*, and this is the starting point for his analysis not only of Faulkner but also of Mauriac, Dos Passos and Albert Camus. Mauriac, by adopting an attitude of God-like omniscience towards his characters, goes against the first rule for writing novels. By depriving Thérèse of her freedom, treating her simply as an example of how divine grace may lurk in the most improbable of souls, he is preventing her from becoming alive. The freedom which characterizes human beings in all their relationships must be respected in art as well as in life, and the only novelists worthy of the name are those whose work is consistent with this vision. 'God is not an artist; neither is Monsieur Mauriac' is the concluding sentence in Sartre's essay, and the beginning of a long but intermittent duel between France's most celebrated Catholic novelist and the writer whom he himself was later to qualify as 'the providential atheist'.[28]

For those whose technique of narration offers either an original vision of human experience or one which fits his own preconceptions, Sartre has the highest praise. The Dos Passos of *1919* is 'the greatest writer of our time' because he makes us realize, by the very way he tells his story, that 'in capitalist society, men do not have lives; they have only destinies'. He thus leads us to rebel, in Sartre's view, not only against the society in which we live, but against the people that we ourselves have become. Camus's decision to write *L'Etranger* in short sentences, avoiding causal constructions and refraining from any explanatory clauses, reflects an absurd world from which all rational connections have disappeared, and this is also a valid way of looking at experience. Sartre may not always agree with what he finds in the authors he admires. 'I admire his art, I don't believe in his metaphysics', he writes of Faulkner, adding the remark that 'a future barred to us nonetheless remains a future'. In July 1939, when this was written, Sartre was living at a time when there seemed to be no viable future for Europeans, and what he says in *Les Mots* about his irrepressible optimism should perhaps be remembered in the context both of this remark and of the accusations of excessive gloom so frequently levelled against him. If it is true that he remained convinced that he had 'a mandate to bear witness for everything', then he would indeed have enjoyed the feeling of invulnerability normally vouchsafed to people with comparable religious or semi-religious convictions.

The essays collected in the first volume of *Situations*, published in book form in 1947 when Sartre was at the height of his fame, are not only a valuable indication of his wide literary tastes and general theory of the novel. They provide autobiographical details, as when he mentions how his maternal grandfather, disappointed in his wife's dowry, lived with her for forty years without saying more than two or three words.[29] His interest in Marxism, considered by some critics to date from the early 1950s, recurs at several points in these essays, and is most noticeable in what is perhaps the rather envious remark that a young worker is compelled to choose for or against Marx.[30] His basic concept of freedom is clearly expressed in the distinction which he makes between minerals and vegetables, whose growth is wholly determined by their environment and genetic structure, and for whom 'obedience is automatic', and man. Because he is free, the only archetype to which man can conform is one which he himself selects, 'perpetually choosing himself to be as he is'.[31] Freedom, Sartre explains in his essay on Descartes, written in 1945, consists not in doing what we want but in wanting to do what we can, and he also finds in Descartes his own view that we know our liberty by the immediate experience which we have of it. Liberty, he also argues in his essay on Mauriac, is not something which can be measured out drop by drop. Men are wholly free or not at all and any attempt to describe or understand human activity has to begin by the recognition of human freedom as the most fundamental of all experiences.

Part II

4 The theatre, philosophy and popularity

i

Although Sartre makes his most autobiographical hero, Mathieu Delarue, take part in a desperate stand against the victorious German armies in June 1940, he himself was taken prisoner without hearing a shot fired in anger. Mathieu did resemble Sartre, however, in serving as a private soldier, and the description in *La Mort dans l'Ame* of how the officers in his regiment abandon their men when they know that defeat is imminent has more interesting implications than the possibly ironical portrait of Mathieu as a Hero of the Last Cartridge. A society whose most intelligent and highly educated members refuse to accept military responsibility has, on purely practical grounds, something seriously wrong with it, and Sartre did later express regret for the anti-militarism which made him refuse to take a commission.[1]

Sartre was a prisoner of war from 21 June 1940 until the end of March 1941. He later said that it was when he was behind barbed wire that he realized what liberty was really like, and he got on quite well with the ordinary peasants and working-men whom he had had little opportunity of meeting in peace time. Even before this fairly crucial experience, however, his ideas had started to change, and when he came on leave in February 1940, Simone de Beauvoir noted that he had begun to conceive his idea of political commitment.[2] In April of the same year, *Le Mur* received the left-wing literary award of the Prix du Roman Populiste, and by Christmas 1940 Sartre had moved even further in the direction of committed literature. By a curious paradox, the work that marked the first stage in his transition was a play on a Biblical theme, written and produced in Stalag XII at Trèves in December 1940. By a treatment of the apocryphal story of Bariona, he was able at one and the same time to speak to his fellow-prisoners about their captivity and suggest to them, by allegory, that all hope of resistance was not lost. He was to repeat this use of allegory in what remained for a long time his first published play, *Les Mouches,* but in other respects *Bariona* remains unique. It is the only one of his plays in which Sartre himself acted one of the parts; and his performance as Balthasar, one of the three kings, was apparently so 'sincere, ardent and burning with faith' that it converted an atheist doctor to Christianity.[3]

Sartre twice insisted, in interviews given long after the first

performance of *Bariona*, that his choice of a subject from what he
called 'Christian mythology' in no way implied that he had ever
wavered in his own atheism.[4] In fact, the play deals only
incidentally with the birth of Christ, and the central issue in the
opening scenes concerns the attitude which Bariona, a village
chieftain in Roman-occupied Palestine, takes towards a demand
for increased taxation. He advocates, to begin with, not passive
resignation but what he calls 'active despair'. By abstaining from
all sexual intercourse with their wives, the men in the village will
create a 'religion of nothingness' that will leave the Romans
only empty, ruined towns. A crisis immediately arises when
Sarah, Bariona's wife, comes to tell him that she is now expecting
the child they had longed for during the long years of their
previously sterile marriage. The rumour that the Messiah has
been born interrupts Bariona's plea that this child should be
killed in its mother's womb, and the villagers go off to Bethlehem.
It is only after a soothsayer has foretold the life and passion of
Christ that Bariona decides to go there too, but with the intention
of killing and not worshipping the infant Jesus. What makes him
change his mind is another speech by Balthasar, one whose theme
is that both the infant Jesus and Bariona's own son will be free,
free to rejoice everlastingly in their own existence and to soar above
the suffering that afflicts the world. Bariona's conversion, in which
he becomes 'Christ's first disciple' immediately results in action.
On learning that Herod and the Romans are coming to kill
Jesus, he leads his villagers in a rearguard action which will
enable Mary, Joseph and the child to escape. In thus leaving the
stage having made up his mind to take part in a war against
oppression and for liberty, Bariona is Sartre's first committed
hero, and the only character in the whole of his work to centre
his action and speeches round an appeal for joy.

Sartre explained in 1968 that his main reasons for not allowing
other performances of his play after its first production at
Christmas 1940 were aesthetic. His remark that it contained
too many long speeches is certainly a valid criticism, and it is
perhaps significant that Sartre's most successful plays, *Huis
Clos* and *Les Mains Sales*, express philosophical or political
ideas through dialogue and action, not through disquisitions.
It is not that *Bariona* wholly lacks dramatic qualities. The
speeches in which the Roman Lelius explains to the Publican
why taxes must be increased show a nice talent for political
satire, and put forward what was in fact the German policy
towards occupied France in terms that could well originally have
applied to first-century Palestine. For all his domestic histrionics,
Charles Schweitzer seems to have given the theatre very little
serious consideration; and it was the success of *Bariona* which
first showed Sartre that the theatre was the best means of

communicating with people who shared the same social or political preoccupations.

It was, consequently, to the theatre that he turned after he had engineered his release from Stalag XII, and the production of *Les Mouches* on 2 June 1943 marked him as the most important literary spokesman for the resistance movement. Simone de Beauvoir describes how Sartre managed to be repatriated by pretending that he had never even been in the army and had consequently been captured by mistake. To prove his unfitness for military service, he showed the German doctor his virtually blind right eye, and forged an entry in his *livret militaire*.[5] He took up his teaching duties again at the Lycée Pasteur, and worked with Maurice Merleau-Ponty in founding a resistance group called Socialisme et Liberté. He went on a cycling tour in the unoccupied part of France in an attempt to recruit new members, but this did not prove very successful. The invasion of Russia had led the French Communist party to abandon the policy of collaboration which it had practised during the first months of the German occupation of France, and Sartre was accused by the Communists, for reasons which seem a little obscure, of having bought his release from the prisoner-of-war camp by agreeing to spy on the resistance movement 'on behalf of the fascist bourgeoisie'.[6] An alternative reason for the failure of Socialisme et Liberté was advanced by Claude Roy when he said that the trouble with all resistance groups run by intellectuals was that everybody wanted to be an officer, and Sartre later contrasted the slight contributions which intellectuals had made to the resistance movement with the much heavier responsibilities assumed by dockers or railwaymen.[7] The only form of resistance open to him was in the writing of *Les Mouches*, and it is as an allegory of the German occupation of France, the Vichy régime and the resistance movement that it is still most obviously meaningful even today.

The story of Orestes, returning to Argos in order to avenge the murder of his father Agamemnon by killing both the usurper Aigisthos and his own mother Clytemnestra, did indeed fit the circumstances of occupied France with an almost uncanny accuracy, and it is difficult to explain why the German censor did not realize what was happening. Perhaps he was less sensitive than right-wing French critics such as Alain Laubreaux and André Castelot to Sartre's attack on the Vichy régime,[8] and the immediate relevance of Sartre's play was in the satire of a purely French attitude. The German victory, argued the Vichy government, was God's way of punishing the French for the wickedness they had shown during the twenties and thirties, when they read Proust and Gide, went on strike for higher wages and holidays with pay, and thought more of the rights involved in *Liberté*,

Egalité, Fraternité than of the duties required by *Travail, Famille, Patrie*. However, such frivolity was now at an end. 'We must suffer and suffer again,' proclaimed Marshal Pétain in his New Year message to the French people in January 1941, 'for we have not yet paid for all our sins,' and this attitude of generalized repentance recurs in *Les Mouches* in the atmosphere which Aigisthos and Clytemnestra spread through Argos. The inhabitants are made to feel perpetually guilty for a crime that they have not committed – the murder of Agamemnon – and spend their lives in an attempt to assuage the anger of the Gods. When Orestes kills both Aigisthos and Clytemnestra he obviously represents the French resistance movement rebelling both against the physical authority of Berlin and the *ordre moral* of Vichy, and there could have been little doubt in the mind of anyone who saw the play in 1943 that it was a profoundly committed work of art.

In an interview given in 1944, Sartre regretted that the censorship should have obliged him to express his ideas in symbolic guise, and described the play which he really ought to have written as 'that of the terrorist who, by shooting Germans in the street, brought about the execution of fifty hostages'.[9] This moral dilemma is not, in fact, all that badly expressed by the drama of a man killing his own mother, and Sartre's choice of the Orestes legend also had important philosophical connotations. In the original legend, Orestes has no choice but to kill Aigisthos and Clytemnestra. The curse on the house of Atreus makes it inevitable that he will avenge his father in this way and be driven mad by the Erinnyes, the goddesses of vengeance which guard the antique law of matriarchal authority. In *Les Mouches*, on the other hand, the most important scene describes the discovery which Orestes makes that he is free to decide whether to follow out his so-called destiny or simply to walk away, and the contrast with the traditional legend is heightened by the change which Sartre makes in the character and function of the Erinnyes. In *Les Mouches*, they are on stage from the very beginning, as the flies which give the play its title and batten on the remorse of the citizens of Argos. The idea which Sartre thus suggests is that the people most afflicted by remorse are those who feel guilty for an act that they did not choose to commit, and this impression is confirmed by the ending which he gives to the play. Because Orestes does have the 'courage of his acts', and 'claims his crime as his own in the full light of the sun',[10] the flies have no power over him. By this acceptance of responsibility, he takes upon himself the 'remorse and nocturnal anguish' of what are now his citizens. He plays a tune on his flute and departs triumphantly from Argos, taking with him the flies of repentance and remorse, just as Browning's Pied Piper took away the rats from Hamelin city.

Like Bariona, he leaves the stage as a man who knows that he has freely taken the right decision, but he does not stay in Argos to help the people to whom he has revealed 'their absurd and tasteless existence, which has been given to them for no purpose'.[11] The implication is that since they too are free, they must face up by themselves to the discovery that human life begins on the far side of despair.

Although it is a remarkably neat illustration of a central thesis in *L'Etre et le Néant*, Sartre's next play was apparently written with purely aesthetic considerations in mind. He had been asked by Marc Barbézat, the printer, to write a play for his wife Olga and for another actress called Wanda. It would have to be easy to produce and take on tour, with no changes of scenery and only three actors. Sartre was also asked to ensure that none of the three actors felt jealous of the two others by being forced to leave the stage and let them have all the best lines; consequently he began to think in terms of a situation where three characters would be locked up together – in a cellar during an air-raid, for example. Suddenly, he hit upon the idea of locking them all up in Hell, and the play was made. Albert Camus had come to the first night of *Les Mouches* and introduced himself to Sartre. He was passionately interested in the theatre, and Sartre asked him if he would like both to produce the play and take the part of Garcin. Camus eventually declined, on the grounds that he was too inexperienced to direct a play for the Parisian stage, and was replaced by a professional director called Raymond Rouleau. *Huis Clos* had its first production in May 1944, at the Théâtre du Vieux Colombier, and its initial run was interrupted by the uprising which drove the Germans out of Paris. It was the first play to be performed in Paris after the Liberation, and its 'second first night', on 20 September 1944, marked the triumph of what was known at the time as *résistentialisme*.

The immediate success of *Huis Clos* offers a microcosm of the mixture between popularity and notoriety which Sartre enjoyed in post-war France. His critics found it morbid; his admirers brilliantly written and morally challenging; and the public at large stimulating as well as occasionally annoying by its metaphysical pretensions. It has, however, continued to prove extremely successful as a play, with countless amateur as well as professional productions to its credit. The gloomy picture which it gives of human relationships is, in fact, ambiguous, and its meaning can vary according to the context in which it is studied. Three people are in Hell, and it is reasonable to assume that they are being punished for something. Garcin, the only man, has based his whole life on the assumption that he was a hero. Yet when the crisis broke and he had to stand by his principles, he ran away. His punishment lies both in his knowledge that the

living will always think of him as a coward, and in the perpetually
haunting possibility that one of the dead with whom he is now
incarcerated, Estelle, might perhaps be persuaded to change
something in this verdict by thinking of him as a brave man. She
would be quite happy to do this, if he would agree to think of her
as the innocent victim of circumstances rather than a frivolous
and immoral woman who murdered her own child. Their exchange
of mutual bad faith would be quite satisfactory were it not for
the third person with them, the lesbian Inès, who has caused her
own and her girl friend's death by a suicide pact, after driving this
girl friend's husband to kill himself. Simply by looking at Garcin
and Estelle, she can use her knowledge of what they are really
like to destroy the complicity between them; and since the first
half of the play has consisted in a general confession, each of the
three people knows just exactly how bad the other two have been.
Their punishment lies in the fact that Garcin's presence will
always destroy the potential affair between Inès and Estelle;
while Estelle's presence will always create rivalry between Inès
and Garcin, preventing the two 'male' characters from establishing
any kind of *modus vivendi*. Meanwhile, the presence of Inès will
always prevent any pact between Garcin and Estelle. The powers
that be, Garcin, realizes, are economizing on manpower. Each
victim is a torturer for the people with him.

In this moral interpretation of the play, Sartre's famous
statement that 'Hell is other people' takes on a fairly precise and
limited meaning. Other people are Hell only in so far as their
presence reminds us of how inadequate our behaviour has been.
If, like Corneille's Rodrigue, we could declare: 'Je le ferais
encore si j'avais à le faire', other people's critical glances would
not matter. We should be able to defy them because we knew
that we had done the right thing, and this is certainly how the
Orestes of *Les Mouches* or the Goetz of *Le Diable et le Bon Dieu*
would act. It is when we read *L'Etre et le Néant* that *Huis Clos* takes
on a much less obviously moral significance. There, Sartre
asserts quite categorically that 'conflict is the original meaning
of myself as I am for other people', that 'my original fall
resides in the existence of other people',[12] and it does seem in this
respect as though the boundary situation described in *Huis Clos*
is privileged in the sense that it reveals the essence of man's
relationship with his fellows. One critic asked whether the
situation would be the same if the three people incarcerated were a
general, a nun and the mother of a family,[13] and it is probable
from Sartre's general attitude towards society that three such
people would be so steeped in bad faith that their mask of
respectability would soon disappear. But even if Che Guevara,
Daniel Cohn-Bendit and Simone de Beauvoir were locked up
together, they would still, according to *L'Etre et le Néant*, be

unable to avoid making their lives a hell. 'Enter not in the judgment of Thy servant, O Lord, for in Thy sight shall no man living be justified' is a phrase that expresses the impossibility for a Christian of ever feeling that he has escaped from the burden of original sin which weighs down even the most virtuous; and Sartre's apparent dismissal, in *L'Etre et le Néant*, of the possibility that anyone should ever have an authentic and positive relationship with his fellows seems to indicate that for him, as for Newman, some 'terrible aboriginal catastrophe' lies at the root of the human adventure. If *L'Etre et le Néant* can be seen as the *summa* of the comprehensive analysis which he offers of the human condition, *Huis Clos* is a kind of instant catechism in which simplified answers are given to a number of basic questions about the nature and destiny of human beings.

It is also an interesting coincidence that the ethic which can be inferred from *Huis Clos* should be as rigorous as any put forward by Calvin, John Knox or the Pascal of the *Provinciales*. 'We don't do what we want and yet we are responsible for what we are' writes Sartre in *Qu'est-ce que la Littérature?*,[14] and the curious mixture, characteristic of extreme Protestantism, between insisting that people do their duty and telling them that they will never attain virtue, is perhaps one of the most troubling features of this play. We have no one to blame but ourselves, and none of the characters can seek refuge in their good intentions; but even a Garcin who had lived up to his own ideals would still be tormented by Inès and Estelle. The production of *Huis Clos* established Sartre as a major dramatist, just as the publication of *La Nausée* had marked him out as an outstanding novelist. A year earlier, in 1943, the appearance of *L'Etre et le Néant* had been greeted by a disconcerting silence. It was not until 1945 that it became the most widely discussed work of contemporary philosophy, and one which had attained, by 1957, its fifty-fifth edition.

ii

At one point in *L'Etre et le Néant*, Sartre repeats an idea previously expressed in *L'Imaginaire* and remarks that a mind which could not 'irrealize' its immediate experience and detach itself from its surroundings would be obliged, when reading a book, to spell out each individual letter without grasping the meaning of the work as a whole.[15] This is perhaps a warning on how not to approach the 722 closely printed pages of *L'Etre et le Néant*, and to offer instead some suggestions on how it might be approached. Alexandre Astruc[16] said that it was as exciting to read as a detective novel, and it is certainly not dull. It is the first pages, with their discussion of the concept of 'nothingness' (*le néant*), which are the most difficult. After them comes a fascinating description of how Sartre thinks that human beings define themselves in relation to the world of physical objects, to other people, and to their past, and how they are perpetually striving towards a mode of being which they are doomed never to attain.

By calling *L'Etre et le Néant* an 'essay in phenomenological ontology', Sartre indicates that he has no metaphysical ambitions, and he remains faithful throughout to the ultimately inexplicable experience which Roquentin has of himself in *La Nausée*. 'The very definition of being', he writes in his conclusion, 'reveals to us its fundamental contingency',[17] and he goes on to say that metaphysical questions as to why this state of affairs should have arisen in the first place are quite meaningless. But although there is no point in speculating about why man is here, it is meaningful to ask questions about what kind of a being he is. It is also the concern of ontology, the study of being, to examine the different ways in which man tries to discover, through his actions, that foundation for his own being which metaphysical enquiry is incapable of producing. Man defines himself, for the Sartre of *L'Etre et le Néant*, by what he is striving to attain, and ontology examines the circumstances in which he finds himself here and now, much as sociology examines what a society is like at the moment. But although Sartre's account of human reality in *L'Etre et le Néant* makes no reference to the past, it does not present a man as a static being. Existential psychoanalysis, declares Sartre, takes over where ontology stops, and perhaps the best way to approach *L'Etre et le Néant* is to concentrate on this idea. It is by looking at why he thinks man should be studied by reference to what he is trying to do that we shall see why his book offers an equally strong challenge to the Freudian, the orthodox Christian and the Marxist.

Sartre defines what he calls 'human reality' – he eschews terms such as 'human nature' as implying that man is to be defined in relation to an already existing archetype – in terms of a longing for a mode of existence apprehended as infinitely desirable but remaining perpetually and tantalizingly out of reach. Yet it is the very quality by which man's mind brings the world into being which creates this perpetual frustration. Without the specifically human activity of asking questions, we could not say that the world as such existed at all. Linguists make a comparable point when they say that the concept 'weed' is comprehensible only in the context of the human activity of growing things deliberately, and what is important is the explanation which Sartre gives of why man should have this ability. It is because he brings with him into the world of solid, massive being, the essential but elusive concept of nothingness. My experience of looking for Peter in a café and finding he is not there – and not there, moreover, in a manner very different from the way in which Wellington or Paul Valéry are not there[18] – is a paradigm case of how man must have the concept of negation if he is going to count, ask questions, doubt, interrogate or plan. But man can only negate, in Sartre's view, by virtue of the fact that he carries a kind of nothingness within himself, as a secret fault which makes all things possible. As soon as he looks at himself and thinks: 'I am me', he realizes that he can do this only because, in some rather peculiar way, he is not quite himself. He is always haunted by the desire to have the absolute solidity which characterizes what Sartre calls the *en-soi*, the in-itself, but is always frustrated. A thin film of nothingness perpetually separates him from himself, making him at one and the same time both conscious of what he is and free. The *en-soi* is neither free nor conscious. It is. A stone cannot say to itself: 'How odd, I'm me'. Neither can it suddenly decide to do something different. For Sartre, man is afraid of this ability to change, but cannot escape from his liberty. He is condemned to be free, just as he is condemned to be conscious. And if anyone doubts this, says Sartre, let him examine his own behaviour and realize how the efforts which he makes to hide his liberty from himself constitute the overwhelming proof that he is free and knows it.

It is thus only because we do not have a transcendent or permanent self that we sometimes pretend not to be free. We use bad faith in order to run away from the anguish which we should otherwise feel at the knowledge that we and we alone are perpetually deciding what kind of person we are, and perpetually bringing moral values into being by what we do. We are not, of course, always fully aware that this is what we are doing. 'Day to day morality excludes ethical anguish',[19] and protects us for most of the time. But once we stop to think, we realize that there is no compelling reason to carry on acting as we do, and it is a form of bad faith akin to Lulu's in *Intimité* for us to pretend that we have been so conditioned that we cannot change. Although Sartre actually wrote the text of *L'Etre et le Néant* between 1940 and 1943, the ideas which he expresses go back much further. *Erostrate* was written in 1936, and the passage on sadism reads like a direct commentary on this story, just as Eve's inability to go mad reflects his view that the *pour-soi* can never escape from its awareness of itself. The Kantian overtones in *L'Imaginaire* also recur in Sartre's discussion of bad faith, for if every one of our actions followed the others with the inevitability of the next step in a well-programmed computer, we should not go to the trouble of pretending that our glands, social conditioning or subconscious drives made certain courses of action either inevitable or impossible.

What distinguishes *L'Etre et le Néant* from Sartre's other work is the fact that the ideas expressed in apparent isolation from one another in the books published before 1943 are welded together in a coherent conceptual framework. He states categorically that it is important 'in ontology, as elsewhere, to maintain a rigorous order',[20] and his use of terms such as *en-soi* and *pour-soi*, his coining of neologisms like 'néantiser' (to nothingize) and the writing of sentences such as 'man is a being who is what he is not and is not what he is'[21] are all essential to his declared aim of providing a comprehensive account of man's present status and basic aim. Knowledge of a partial or empirical kind is, he writes, 'meaningless' as far as ontology is concerned, and it is perhaps inevitable that a system which is meant to be comprehensive (*totalitaire*) should bring with it a specialized vocabulary and some linguistic peculiarities. Elsewhere, Sartre explains the title of his book by saying that, 'coming to the study of human reality from a new point of view',[22] he always finds the same 'indissoluble couple' of being and nothingness, and *L'Etre et le Néant* is written with the self-assurance of a man convinced that he has hit upon truths which have evaded all other thinkers. Since, however, a comprehensive system is by definition one which remains the same however one walks about in it, it is justifiable to follow a different order from the one Sartre claims to be necessary, selecting aspects which show it in a slightly different light. Central to his vision of man as constantly free to choose himself and permanently aware of what he is doing is his rejection of the subconscious. It is also this which is essential to the challenge which his concept of existential psychoanalysis offers to the theories of Freud.

There is one aspect of traditional psychoanalysis that Sartre does accept: the idea that man 'expresses his whole personality in the most insignificant and superficial things he does, that there is not a taste, not a *tic*, not a human action which is not significant'.[23] For Sartre, as for the Freud of *The Psycho-Pathology of Everyday Life*, we do not forget names or mix up the order of words in a sentence because of a mechanical fault in our speech system. There is an underlying reason for everything we do, however trivial it might appear. Where Sartre parts company with Freud is in his rejection of the subconscious. On purely logical grounds, he argues, the concept of psychic censorship is self-contradictory. The mind can repress certain tendencies only if it recognizes them for what they are. But these tendencies are then no longer unconscious, and the mind can no more act in this way than a teacher can tell a boy he does not know is there to shut up. Sartre further argues that the importance which Freudians attach to the resistance shown by the patient when the final cure is about to take place is comprehensible only if the complex has existed all along in the conscious mind. Why, he asks, should the patient fear the revelation of something which he does not even know exists? His resistance is explicable only by the concept of bad faith. This alone can explain why the patient should have chosen a particular complex to avoid his sense of freedom, and why he should be so reluctant to recognize what he has been doing. The diagnosis of the various forms of bad faith will clearly be one of the main tasks of any existential psychoanalysis stemming from *L'Etre et le Néant*. This will not, however, be its only task, and the fact that Sartre twice mentions biography as the field in which this technique will show its paces, promising to give two examples by studying Flaubert and Dostoyevsky, suggests that it might have literary rather than clinical application.

This impression, however, is not entirely accurate. In June 1947, Sartre read a paper to the Société Française de Philosophie entitled 'Conscience de soi et Connaissance de soi'. There, he repeated his argument in *L'Etre et le Néant* that we have, for most of the time, what he calls a 'non-thetic' awareness of ourselves and not an 'analytical and detailed' one. In *L'Etre et le Néant* he writes that the mind is 'penetrated by a great light without being able to express what this light illuminates',[24] and while it is not very easy to see quite how this distinction between self-knowledge and self-awareness can be maintained, it is one that he observes consistently. In his paper to the philosophical society, he also argued that the concept of the unconscious had no practical application in clinical analysis, and claimed that there were analysts already using methods more in keeping with his own ideas. He did not, however, reveal any names, and it is in England rather than in France that existential psychoanalysis has been developed, notably by R. D. Laing and R. M. Cooper. *Les Mots* is perhaps not consistent with his remark in *L'Etre et le Néant* that no one can use this method of analysis on himself, but Sartre's concentration, in his books on Baudelaire, Genet and Flaubert, on what the French call 'l'âge de raison', the period between the ages of seven and nine when a child is considered to be able to judge the moral implications of his acts, is another important departure from Freudian principles. What matters for the Freudians is what happens to a child between the ages of three and five, when the Oedipus complex is at its height. What occurs then is the incident which, according to Sartre, the Freudians see as crucial in determining the child's development, and he seeks to replace this by the idea of a conscious choice taken a few years later. What this free choice expresses, however, is not a random or an undefined desire. It reflects the basic attitude which the individual adopts towards the *pour-soi* that he is and the *en-soi-pour-soi* that he would like to be. It is at this point that the concept of existential psychoanalysis links up with the general picture of human reality given in the rest of *L'Etre et le Néant*, and that the difference between Sartre and Freud epitomizes two totally incompatible visions of how the mind works.

For Sartre, the *pour-soi*, or human mind, contains nothing. Indeed, in a way, it is nothing but a force immediately conscious of itself and of the world, a force which knows its capacity for change and self-denial and wishes to escape from it. But it does not wish, in escaping, to lose its self-awareness, and longs rather for that moment when it will coincide as absolutely with itself as the *en-soi* does, while still retaining that self-awareness which the *en-soi* lacks. This is, Sartre repeats throughout *L'Etre et le Néant*, a self-defeating and self-contradictory ambition, and at one point he actually compares the human mind to a donkey induced to pull a cart by having a carrot dangled in front of its nose, but finding that by moving the cart it prevents itself from getting the carrot.[25] It nevertheless is this longing for the repose and justification offered by the a-temporal and conscious coincidence of self with self which lies at the heart of all human endeavour; and it is this that existential psychoanalysis must examine if it is to satisfy what Sartre describes, in *Saint Genet, Comédien et Martyr*, as his own 'passion for understanding mankind'.[26]

Since human beings are perpetually aware of themselves as lacking something, the various activities whereby we seek to possess the world deserve special attention, and Sartre offers a brilliant analysis of how I symbolically appropriate a stretch of virgin snow by ski-ing over it again and again.[27] Elsewhere he writes that 'filling up holes is, in its original meaning, making a sacrifice of my body so that the fullness of being might exist, that is to say I am undergoing the passion of the *Pour-soi* to mould, complete and save the totality of the *En-soi*.'[28] One of the most fundamental tendencies of human reality is to fill up gaps, and the child who sucks his thumb is trying to 'dilute it and transform it into a sticky paste that will block up the hole constituted by his mouth'.[29] Peculiar though these two particular examples may be, they nevertheless express what Sartre insists is the true picture of how and why human beings behave as they do. Just as he argued, in his first article on Husserl and in his books on the imagination, that it is wrong to conceive the mind as a container filled with a collection or succession of perceptions, images, desires and fears, so he maintains in *L'Etre et le Néant* that people are not moved to act by forces such as Love, Ambition, Fear, the Libido or the Lust for Power. These may well be useful concepts for analysing at a fairly superficial level the way that some people behave, but they do not lead to the deepest and most satisfactory explanation. The longing to make the *pour-soi* and *en-soi* coincide is more fundamental than any of these, and even the sexual impulse is only a form which this longing takes. As against what he sees as the Freudian view of man driven hither and thither by the sexual impulses that exist like indomitable forces within him, Sartre puts up his own view of man as defined by the aims rather than the content of his mind.

Man's desire to attain this total coincidence of self with self is frequently described, in *L'Etre et le Néant*, in a religious vocabulary which lends weight to the views of those who see Sartrean existentialism as a kind of perverted, neo-Jansenistic Christianity. Indeed, when Sartre writes that the phrase about God being 'sensible au coeur'[30] (apprehended by the heart) is a correct description of the way man feels that God represents his highest ideal, he comes remarkably close to Pascal; while his insistence on man's perpetual inability to attain this ideal is oddly reminiscent of Kierkegaard's remarks about the 'infinite and qualitative difference between God and man'. Sartre differs from the Christian existentialists, however, in his view that man actually wants to be God, not simply to believe in Him, and his atheism is perhaps even more visible in his statement that the very concept of God as a being which is *Ens causa sui*, an *en-soi-pour-soi* beyond contingency, is contradictory. Since this is so, man's attempt to 'lose himself in order that God may be born' transforms him into a 'useless passion', a being who perpetually seeks to sacrifice himself for a will o' the wisp that cannot ever conceivably exist. The Catholic journal *La Croix* denounced existentialism, on 3 July 1945, as 'a more serious danger than eighteenth-century rationalism or nineteenth-century positivism', and while it is difficult to imagine anyone being dissuaded from a belief in God by the arguments put forward in *L'Etre et le Néant*, the hostility which the more orthodox and authoritarian Christian apologists feel towards Sartre is readily comprehensible. He even offers the ultimate insult of using a specifically Christian vocabulary and precise Biblical references to illustrate some of his ideas, and writes that 'my original sin' is my emergence into a world where other people exist.[31] The moment when Adam and Eve knew that they were naked and hid themselves illustrates how we realize that other people must exist because of the feelings of shame which we all have, and Sartre's whole analysis of human relationships accepts as inevitable a state of permanent hostility that completely contradicts the Christian injunction to 'love one another'. His argument that man is totally free and totally responsible for creating his own moral values also strikes at the very heart of a religion where ethical values are held to have been revealed to man by God, and where perfect freedom lies only in His service.

Sartre's view of religion as alienation clearly brings him close

to Marx, and his insistence on the inevitability of conflict is
also consistent with the statement in the *Communist Manifesto*
that all history is the history of class struggle. What he criticizes
in Marxism, however, is what he calls the bad faith of the men
who escape from their anguish by believing that there are
pre-established values 'inscribed in the clear heavens'.[32] By
regarding their activity as sanctioned, in the last resort, by the
inevitable process of history, the Marxists are victims of what
Sartre calls the 'esprit de sérieux'. They believe that clearly
defined tasks await them in their progress through life with the
same inevitability that milestones await the traveller on certain
roads, and thereby miss the truth enunciated by Orestes when he
tells Electra that 'every man must invent his own way'. Moreover,
when Sartre goes on from his criticism of the Marxist 'esprit de
sérieux' to say that the principal task of existential psychoanalysis
will be to make people realize that no human activity is in any
way privileged, he is clearly issuing a direct challenge. The
Marxist is no more able than the Christian to agree that there is
'no difference between sitting and getting drunk in a room by
oneself and going out to be a leader among men', and even less
that the 'quietism of the lone tippler may perhaps carry the
day over the vain agitation of the Leader of the People'.[33] It is
unlikely, on purely chronological grounds, that a little man from
the French Communist Party sat in his dirty raincoat and read
through *L'Etre et le Néant*, jumped to his feet when he read on
page 669 that 'Marx set out the first dogma of *le sérieux* when he
affirmed the priority of the object over the subject', and sent off a
pigeon denouncing Sartre as a fascist spy. By 1944, Communist
hostility had in fact relented to the point where Sartre got on
quite well with the party members on the Conseil National
d'Écrivains, and it was not until after the Liberation that they
began to accuse him of making man walk on all fours. Nevertheless
his major attack on communist ideology in 'Matérialisme et
Révolution', published in *Les Temps Modernes* in June and July
1946, stems directly from a passage in *L'Etre et le Néant* in which
he argues that hunger and unhappiness do not create revolutions
in the same way that heat makes water boil. Only free minds,
examining and judging the present situation in the light of
present desires and future possibilities, can develop the idea of
a revolution. This rejection of Marxist determinism was to remain
for a long time the most important philosophical difference between
Sartre and the highly orthodox French Communist Party.

iii

If *L'Etre et le Néant* had to wait longer than Sartre's other works
before making any great impact on the reading public, he more than

made up for it after the war by his ability to exploit both traditional means of literary expression and the newly liberated mass media. Indeed, he seemed almost to rejoice at the way his philosophy exactly fitted the mood of the time, and wrote in 1944 that the German occupation had compelled men to face up to the realities of exile, captivity and death which characterized 'this desperate, unbearable situation called the human condition'.[34] Between 1940 and 1944, he continued, Frenchmen had known that they might be captured and tortured by the Germans. If this happened, they would find themselves totally alone and totally responsible, confronted with the essence of human liberty: the power to create the values of courage and loyalty by saying no; the terror of betraying humanity itself by yielding to their torturers. They would, in fact, be in exactly the kind of position which existentialist philosophy depicted as being most typically human, and it is remarkable how a style of thinking which had begun, as far as Sartre was concerned, with an academic enquiry into the workings of the imagination, should have come to express what Claude Roy called in 1946 'up-to-date common sense'.[35]

The theme of torture recurs with almost obsessional insistence in Sartre's work, and in November 1946 he made his first attempt to express through literature some of the moral and psychological problems which it raised. The production of *Morts sans Sépulture*, as part of a double bill with *La Putain Respectueuse*, enjoyed a considerable *succès de scandale* as well as evoking a violent hostility which Simone de Beauvoir explains by the fact that 'the bourgeoisie was closing its ranks and found it bad taste to reawaken unpleasant memories'.[36] Many of the protests were directed against Sartre's defiance of the canons of French classical taste by putting torture scenes on the stage, but even after these had been drastically cut, the play was still not a success. The flip side has proved much more popular, and the story of the golden-hearted whore who sells a Negro down the river because she has too great a respect for the official values of American society, has been repeated innumerable times as a double feature with *Huis Clos*. As Gabriel Marcel rather tartly observed, the play was not a very nice bread-and-butter letter for Sartre to send after the welcome he had received on his first visit to the States in January 1945, and after so many Americans had died liberating Europe. However, Sartre did better for his Russian public. When the play was produced in Moscow in 1954, he gave it a happy ending by making Lizzie grab a revolver and help the Negro fight his would-be lynchers.[37]

The extent of Sartre's post-war notoriety can perhaps be judged by the fact that *une respectueuse* soon became the slang word for a prostitute,[38] and by 1946 Saint Germain-des-Prés had quite ousted Montparnasse as the place where bad American

tourists went – generally in vain – to find good French writers.
Sartre lived for a time at the Hôtel de la Louisiane, and the news
that he had been stricken with mumps and was being nursed by
the actress Marie-Olivier attracted considerable attention from
the journalists of *France-Dimanche*.[39] M. Mancy, Anne-Marie
Schweitzer's second husband, had died in January 1945, and in
1946 Sartre went to live with his mother in the rue Bonaparte,
still within a stone's throw of the Café de Flore. Madame Mancy
proved a willing hostess for the large circle of friends that her
son now enjoyed, and one passage in Simone de Beauvoir's
La Force de l'Age draws an idyllic picture of her making
toffee apples for the team of writers and journalists working with
Sartre on *Les Temps Modernes*. The first number of this review,
named after the Charlie Chaplin film *Modern Times*, had appeared
in October 1945, with Sartre writing in his *Présentation* that he
'held Flaubert and the Goncourt brothers responsible for the
repression that followed the Commune because they had not
written a line to prevent it'.[40] The analytical approach, which
according to Sartre had characterized the bourgeoisie during its
struggle for power and long reign, had outlived its time. Its only
possible function nowadays was to 'trouble the revolutionary
spirit', and it had consequently to be replaced by an attempt at
synthesis which would study man as a dynamic whole, while at
the same time urging him to commit himself deliberately to the
class and epoch to which he belonged. Intellectually, the aim of
Les Temps Modernes was thus to constitute a 'synthetic anthro-
pology', building up that comprehensive knowledge of man which
Sartre had begun to sketch out in *L'Etre et le Néant*. Socially,
it was to contribute to the liberation of mankind by providing a
forum in which writers could study and take sides on various
issues. Sartre made a point of insisting that there was no fixed
party line, but the record of his review has in fact been one of
steady and increasing support for the left.

W. H. Auden's remark that Freud incarnated 'a whole climate
of opinion' is applicable to Sartre as much for the impact which
Les Temps Modernes has made in France as for the ideas which his
literary and philosophical work has put into world-wide
circulation. In post-war France, Sartre also made good use of
the press to expound his views, and there was even, in October
and November 1946, a brief period in which the French radio
let *Les Temps Modernes* have its own programme. However,
this soon had to be suspended because of the violent polemics
to which it gave rise. A *mise au point* published in the
Communist newspaper *Action* on 29 December 1944 is, like the
lecture 'L'Existentialisme est un Humanisme', a useful summary
of Sartre's most widely discussed ideas in post-war France, and
the fact that he begins both the article and the lecture by referring

to the violent attacks made against him indicates the extent to which he had become a *cause célèbre*. Man alone, he argues, is free to create his essence by the acts which he performs. It is therefore natural for us to feel anguish at the idea that each one of our acts, even when we do not wish it, creates not only 'the man that we would like to be ourselves' but also 'an image of man such as we think he ought to be'. This idea, shorn of its more dramatic associations, has close similarities to the Kantian injunction: 'Act as if the maxim of your action were to become through your will a general natural law', and one of the reasons why Sartre later declared the lecture 'L'Existentialisme est un Humanisme' to have been 'a mistake'[41] was perhaps a fear that his new philosophy, if oversimplified, might be assimilated to a more conventional and better established ethical system. The circumstances under which this lecture was delivered, on the evening of 29 October 1945, are again an indication of the vogue enjoyed by Sartrean existentialism in post-war France. The room at the Club Maintenant was so full that fifteen people fainted, and there was such a commotion that thirty chairs were broken. The paradox of the triumph which Sartre enjoyed in his and the century's forties was that it fulfilled all his ambitions but at the wrong time. Charles Schweitzer had firmly convinced him, in his childhood, that no writer worth his salt is ever famous until long after his death. Sartre, on the other hand, was so well known that he achieved the rare but enviable distinction of being condemned, within the same year, by both the Catholic Church and the Communist Party. On 30 October 1948, his whole work was placed upon the Index; and in December, a man called Fadeiev, speaking at a Peace Conference in Poland, compared him to a jackal with a typewriter and a hyena with a fountain pen.[42]

5 Commitment, essays and novels

i

The publication of *Qu'est-ce que la Littérature?* first in review form in *Les Temps Modernes* in 1947, and later as a book in 1948, added to Sartre's notoriety by the challenge which it offered to his fellow writers and the offence which it gave to other literary and political groups. The followers of Surrealism, who still insisted on considering themselves as representing a revolutionary avant-garde, were dismissed with almost as much scorn as the more conservative figures in the French literary establishment; while Sartre's remark that 'the policy of Stalinist communism is incompatible with the honest exercise of the literary profession'[1] typified the violent attack which he launched throughout *Qu'est-ce que la Littérature?* on a party which he accused of stifling the revolution in order better to serve the foreign policy of the Soviet Union, and of teaching a Marxist philosophy which had been 'degraded into a stupid materialism'. His apparent thesis that only committed literature was either worth writing or deserved reading drew strong protests from critics who wished to save literature from being taken over by politics, while his remark that because Molière's satire was directed solely against those who did not conform, it was 'less courageous and much harsher' than the 'great satire' of Beaumarchais, Paul-Louis Courrier, Jean Vallès and Céline,[2] showed how far he was prepared to go in reversing traditional judgments. 'It appears that bananas', he wrote, 'taste better when eaten straight off the tree. The works of the mind, similarly, should be consumed on the spot'.[3] It seemed to many critics that the corollary to this argument was that no book would be worth reading more than a few years after its publication, and when Sartre wrote in an explanatory text 'Ecrire pour son époque', published in *Les Temps Modernes* in June 1948, that '*L'Emile* or *Les Lettres Persanes* had to be read when they had just been gathered',[4] the distinction between literature and journalism seemed quite to have disappeared.

Until the publication of *Les Mots*, the idea that *Qu'est-ce que la Littérature?* might be directed against Sartre himself seemed highly improbable. Nevertheless, when Sartre declares that the writing of books should not be considered as an attempt to 'tear oneself away from life in order to contemplate Platonic essences in a world at rest',[5] the very terms employed anticipate his description and rejection, in *Les Mots*, of the vision imparted to him by Charles Schweitzer. In this, writers and artists did indeed live in an ivory tower, 'meditating on Beauty and Goodness' and maintaining spiritual values by contemplating 'the impossible Ideas',[6] and if the dates which Sartre gives in *Les Mots* for the various stages through which he subsequently passed in his attitude towards literature are correct, he may well have been 'thinking against himself' when he devoted *Qu'est-ce que la Littérature?* to denouncing this idealistic and unworldly concept of the writer's calling. When asked, in 1964, whether he really did mean that it was not until 1952 or so that he began to abandon the semi-religious vision of literature described in *Les Mots*, he replied that this was indeed the case.[7] His change of attitude, he added, could be attributed to an evolution in his relationship with the Communist Party which did not take place until the early 1950s, six or seven years after the publication of *Qu'est-ce que la Littérature?* This is hard to swallow when one reads in the *Présentation des 'Temps Modernes'*, in October 1945, that 'posthumous glory is always based upon a misunderstanding', in *Qu'est-ce que la Littérature?* itself, in 1947, that 'the function of the writer is to ensure that no one can avoid knowing what is happening and therefore claim innocence', and in 'Ecrire pour son Epoque', in June 1948, that 'we are for an ethic and an art of the finite'.

Whatever the relationship of *Qu'est-ce que la Littérature?* may be to Sartre's childhood vision of himself as an unknown writer devoting all his energies to the disinterested maintenance of eternal spiritual values, the essay does have close links with the ideas and ambitions he was actually expressing in the 1940s. When he writes that the aim of art is to 'recuperate this world by presenting it as it is but as if it had its source in human liberty',[8] he is proposing a more dynamic solution than Roquentin's to the problem of contingency. When he complains that he and the committed writers like him have 'readers but not a public' because the proletariat is virtually held prisoner by the Communist Party while the bourgeoisie has taken on that 'amorphous and gelatinous aspect which characterizes oppressed classes before they become conscious of their condition'[9] he is not only using his favourite adjectives in a context where they might at first sight seem a shade irrelevant. He is referring back with nostalgia to the period when he would like to have lived, the eighteenth century, that 'rapidly lost paradise of the French writer', when Voltaire, Diderot, Rousseau and the *Encyclopédistes* represented at one and the same time the cause of freedom and the interests of the rising class. The problem for Sartre, as his attack on the Communist Party in *Qu'est-ce que la Littérature?* makes clear, is that the new rising class, the proletariat, is represented in France by a party that has no interest in liberty. Partly as a result of this, Sartre is forced to acknowledge that the only possible public for writers like himself is the bourgeoisie, and he comments somewhat wryly on what has been, since the middle of the nineteenth century, the main paradox of the progressive writer: in all advanced works of art, the middle class is held up as the enemy, and its values treated with contempt; yet it is almost exclusively members of this class who buy the books, pictures and theatre tickets which enable both rebellious and revolutionary artists to keep alive.

Sartre's view that literature ought to aim at being 'the subjective self-awareness of a society in permanent revolution'[10] leads him virtually to rewrite the history of French literature in such a way as to show that its greatest period was indeed the eighteenth century. This naturally gives his book a very lopsided air, and it is also very parochial. It mentions neither Shakespeare, Goethe, Tolstoy nor Dante, and assumes that the distinction elaborated by French symbolist poets in the nineteenth century between prose as communication and poetry as the use of language purely for its own sake applies to all poets everywhere. 'Between these two acts of writing', proclaims Sartre, 'the only common factor is the movement of the hand tracing the characters',[11] and it would be interesting to have had the views of Browning or Tennyson on this point. There are some other nice touches of involuntary humour, as when Sartre doubts whether America has a middle class, or thinks of all English writers as safely ensconsed in their clubs,[12] and it is a very stimulating book to read. Its central defect does not lie in its plea for committed literature. There have been good books written on social issues, and there is no reason why authors should not express political views in their novels or plays if they wish to do so. But *Anna Karenina, Right-Ho Jeeves, Hamlet* and *Gone with the Wind* are all rightly classified by public libraries as 'literature', and no theorizing, however ingenious or stimulating, can stand up for a moment unless it begins by recognizing this fact. Sartre's does not, and his excessively narrow vision may have sprung from his automatic transference into the field of literary criticism of the theory of reading put forward in *L'Imaginaire*. It is his insistence that the mind can imagine only if it is free which leads him to declare, in *Qu'est-ce que la Littérature?*, that 'the writer, a free man addressing other free men, has only one subject: liberty . . . The art of prose belongs to the only régime where prose can have a meaning: democracy',[13] and there is only one flaw in this impeccably argued, generous ideal: some of the best prose in French literature was written by Pascal and Bossuet. It is, however, also possible to trace back the strident over-simplifications of *Qu'est-ce que la Littérature?* to Sartre's upbringing. If he had not had one exclusive view of literature drilled into him before the age of ten, he would not have come out with an opposite but equally absolutist vision in his forties. Neither would a sensibly educated Jean-Paul have proclaimed, as Sartre did in 1960, 'If literature is not everything, it is nothing.'[14] But then if Kierkegaard had been sensibly brought up, Christian existentialism might never have existed.

ii

The outcry provoked by *Qu'est-ce que la Littérature?* was to some extent a repetition of the attacks made on Sartre when his essay on Baudelaire, first published in 1946 as a preface to Baudelaire's *Ecrits Intimes*, appeared in book form early in 1947. Sartre was accused of neither liking nor understanding poetry, and 'Yéfime', reviewing the book in the conservative *Mercure de France*, remarked that Sartre's critical method would have been just as valid if Baudelaire had shown performing fleas in public and scratched himself in private.[15] This is not altogether fair, partly because Sartre does have some very perceptive things to say about Baudelaire's poetry, but more particularly because he is not directly concerned with *Les Fleurs du Mal*. Baudelaire wrote his *Ecrits Intimes* – *Fusées*, and *Mon Coeur Mis à Nu* – fairly late in life, at a time when the self-pity which already mars the early poem, *Bénédiction*, had turned into a misanthropic and reactionary pessimism which even the most enthusiastic admirers of his poetry find difficult to accept. The concluding sentence in Sartre's book – 'the free choice which a man makes of himself coincides absolutely with what is called his destiny' – summarizes his principal thesis: that Baudelaire deliberately chose solitude, unhappiness and rejection because this was the easiest way in which he could make sense of his experience. It is both an advantage and a drawback of Sartre's approach that he cannot be proved either right or wrong; and although his implied recommendation that we should examine our conduct before blaming either other people or our fate is certainly healthier and more attractive than Baudelaire's sweeping statements in the *Ecrits Intimes* about the wickedness of humanity in general, and of the Belgians in particular, it is also rather easily parodied. Thus it is quite obvious, in *Le Sursis*, that Philippe Grésigne is a fictional portrait of Baudelaire, and the transposition of Baudelaire's affaire with Jeanne Duval into an episode where Philippe is seduced by a prostitute from Martinique who keeps him prisoner in her room by hiding his trousers is very amusing. However, when Philippe's stepfather, Général Lacaze, catches up with him and tells him that 'Even to do evil, you need to be a man . . . you need will-power and perseverance',[16] the schoolmasterish aspect of Sartrean ethics becomes rather visible. It is not quite George Saintsbury saying that what Rousseau's hero, Saint-Preux, needed was a good public school education, but it is not far off.

It is inevitable that one should look to Sartre's own work

for examples of successfully committed literature, and probable that his plays, and especially *Les Séquestrés d'Altona*, offer the best example of how he puts his theories into practice. The essay *Réflexions sur la Question Juive*, however, published in book form in November 1946, also satisfies some of the requirements of *Qu'est-ce que la Littérature?*, especially in being concerned with a problem which was then at the forefront of everybody's mind. The attempt by the Nazis to exterminate the whole Jewish people, and the support given to the anti-semitic policies of the Germans by the Vichy government, had given the whole question of anti-semitism an even greater urgency than it had had in 1939, when Sartre put forward the basic thesis of the first part of his essay in the short story, *L'Enfance d'un Chef*.

A letter which Sartre wrote to the Jewish student review *Hillel* in December 1945 indicated that he had, at the request of certain Jewish friends, agreed to omit the second, more controversial part of his essay from its publication in review form,[17] and it is true that while almost everyone agreed with the main points that Sartre made in his portrait of the anti-semite, his views on what he termed 'Jewish authenticity' proved much less acceptable. Indeed, it is so obvious that anti-semitism is a means whereby the mediocre try to escape from their feelings of inferiority by inventing a scapegoat, that Sartre's use of his theory about man's 'profound inconsistency' and desire to 'transform himself into a stone' is not really necessary to his diagnosis.[18] Of course, the first part of the essay is not perfect, and Sartre later admitted that by limiting himself to a 'phenomeno-logical description' – an attempt to 'elucidate the essence' of the anti-semite by examining him as he is here and now – he had not given sufficient weight to historical and economic factors.[19] But although these might have led him to reconsider his view that anti-semitism is not found among the working class, and to give more importance to the vision of the Jews as the murderers of Christ which inspired much mediaeval anti-semitism,[20] his basic thesis would not have needed to be altered. Epigrams such as 'if the Jew did not exist, the anti-semite would invent him' help to make the *Réflexions* one of his most immediately accessible and stimulating works, and it is not surprising either that it was the second volume to be included in 1961 in Gallimard's highly successful *Collection d'Idées*, immediately after Camus's *Le Mythe de Sisyphe*, or that it had, by 1967, sold 185,000 copies.[21]

The recommendation in the second part of the essay that the Jew should accept his situation as 'a man whom other men think of as a Jew', thus deriving his authenticity from this free choice of himself in his immediate situation, has been much less widely accepted. It runs parallel to Sartre's view that the worker attains his authenticity when he chooses to become a revolutionary, to his admiration for the Negro who 'picks up the word "nigger" that is thrown at him like a stone and proudly proclaims himself as black in the face of the white man', as well as to his praise of André Gide, in *Baudelaire*, for having accepted his homosexuality and built his own ethical system upon it.[22] However, Sartre does not cast it in a very tactful or obvious form. He offends all forms of Judaism by denying that Jews can be defined by their religion, and also rejects the idea that there is such a thing as a Jewish race. He also has little time for what is perhaps the most viable form of Jewish authenticity, the rationalism which rejects racial distinctions and sees all men as united by their common humanity, and the attitude he recommends has an obvious similarity with the ideology of the various Black Power groups in the United States. Sartre himself would argue, however, that there is a fundamental difference between the racialism of an authentic Negro or an authentic Jew, and the racialism of an ardent supporter of Apartheid. He insists in *Qu'est-ce que la Littérature?* that a good novel could never be written in favour of anti-semitism because an ideology which denies liberty to one group of people contradicts the essentially open and democratic nature of literature; and he would criticize a repressive racialism for trying to deprive men of that freedom which alone makes them human. Indeed, he claims that 'it is possible to imagine that a good novel could be written by an American Negro, even if it is overflowing with hatred for the whites, since what he is demanding through this hatred is the liberty of his race',[23] and he obviously sees racialism as good or bad according to the person adopting it. The appeal for an open society honestly based upon the recognition that conflict is inevitable is fundamental both to *Qu'est-ce que la Littérature?* and the *Réflexions sur la Question Juive*, and the extension of the Sartrean concept of authenticity to the field of race relations makes this essay one of the most obviously contemporary of all his works. In this respect, of course, one might regret that some bananas are so long in losing their taste.

iii

The impression which Sartre gave, immediately after the Liberation, of virtually dominating the French literary scene, did not come solely from the obvious applicability of his ideas to a period when all possibilities, temporarily at least, did seem to be open. He was also publishing books which had been completed some time earlier, but which had had to wait for a more propitious moment. The first volume of *Les Chemins de la Liberté*, *L'Age de Raison*, had been ready for publication since 1939, and the second volume, *Le Sursis*, since early 1943.[24] However, since the plot of the first centred round the efforts made by a philosophy teacher, Mathieu Delarue, to find the money needed to pay for his mistress to have an abortion, it would never have been passed by the censor in the atmosphere of *ordre moral* maintained by the Vichy government. And since the second described the Munich agreement of September 1938 as an *assassinat historique*,[25] it would not have been welcomed by a government committed to the view that the German conquest of France was providential. The plot of *L'Age de Raison* shows interesting similarities to Bariona's original idea of how the Romans might best be defied, and also perhaps justifies François Mauriac's later description of Sartre as a 'bachelor novelist whose characters have so curious an obsession with abortion'.[26] Certainly, the appearance of both novels in the spring and early summer of 1945 added to Sartre's notoriety as well as to his reputation, and he found it necessary to defend the plot of *L'Age de Raison*, by saying in an interview 'in 1938, abortion was pursued as a crime. It must therefore have existed.'[27]

The ironic overtones of the title *L'Age de Raison* might perhaps be better rendered if it were translated *Years of Discretion*, for Sartre certainly is talking about the lack of maturity of his main character rather than the possibility of his living in the atmosphere of the seventeenth or eighteenth century. It is much more obviously a work of fiction than *La Nausée*, and its almost over-dramatic plot culminates in the scene where the homosexual, Daniel, finally removes the need for an abortion by suddenly announcing that he is going to marry Marcelle. He feels that by perpetually reminding himself, by the horror which Marcelle's over-abundant and fertile flesh will inspire in him, of how much he prefers men and detests himself, he will come closer to grasping his own homosexuality as the very core of his being. His aim, as he says in *Le Sursis*, is 'to be a homosexual as an oak-tree is an oak-tree',[28] and he is perhaps the character in *Les Chemins de la Liberté* who most clearly illustrates the ideas of *L'Etre et le Néant*. He is also brilliantly depicted, and the brief glimpses which we have of him in *Le Sursis*, fulfilling his own ironic observation that everybody knows what ideal husbands homosexuals make, are very funny.[29] Mathieu comes off less successfully, largely because he is so obviously an anti-hero. He never does or says anything intelligent, and emerges from the two or three discussions he has with his brother Jacques, a conventional and successful lawyer who is obviously meant to be taken as yet another bourgeois *salaud*, as a half-baked intellectual with a thoroughly inconsistent set of ideas. He is no more successful in answering the moral objections which his brother formulates against abortion than he is in defending his readiness to abandon his anti-militarism and go to war in 1938 in order to defend Czechoslovakia, and it is difficult to see quite how Sartre expects his reader to react to these scenes. A similar problem arises when Mathieu says to himself, at the end of *L'Age de Raison*, 'it all seemed so natural, so normal: he was a bastard, Daniel was a homosexual, that was the way things were (*c'était dans l'ordre des choses*).'[30] In scenes like this, Sartre reaches heights of apparently unintentional self-parody which are all the more surprising when one remembers how successful he was in satirizing the ideas of l'Autodidacte in *La Nausée* or Monsieur Darbédat's attitude in *La Chambre*.

Except for the fact that he is tall and broad-shouldered, Mathieu is clearly Sartre himself, with his passion for the cinema, his large hands, the impression he gives people of never having had a childhood, and his ignorance of English. His remark that 'if I did not try to assume my existence on my own account, it would seem so absurd to me to exist' is also, like his passionate resolve to be free, a reflection of Sartre's own major philosophical preoccupations.[31] Although Sartre seems never to have completed the four volumes originally planned, the brief account which Simone de Beauvoir gives of how the plot of the last volume, *La Dernière Chance*, was intended to end also suggests that Mathieu represented a certain degree of wish fulfilment as well. He is not killed in his last stand against the Germans, is taken prisoner, and joins an organization which helps French soldiers to escape. His friend Brunet meets up with him again just as Mathieu is taking part in the execution of a suspected traitor, and he has clearly lost some of the moral scruples which earlier prevented him from acting effectively. After he escapes from captivity himself, he shares with Odette – his brother's wife, who clearly fancies him throughout the first three volumes – what Simone de Beauvoir calls 'the fullness of a shared passion'. This happiness, however, is short-lived. Mathieu is captured by the Gestapo and dies under torture, 'heroic not by essence' – again as Simone de Beauvoir puts it – but because 'he had made himself a hero'.[32] Sartre's failure to complete this rather edifying ending fits in very well with the banana theory in *Qu'est-ce que la Littérature?*, for the problems of the Resistance and Occupation rapidly began to lose their actuality in post-war France. Nevertheless, it is disappointing that Sartre did not complete his tetralogy, especially since he seems to make rather a habit of not carrying his most interesting projects through to their conclusion. Like the biography of Dostoyevsky, the book on ethics referred to in a footnote to the closing pages of *L'Etre et le Néant* has never appeared. *Les Communistes et la Paix*, Sartre's most ambitious piece of political journalism, was never officially completed, and the second volume of *La Critique de la Raison Dialectique* seems, like the final version of his essay on Flaubert, to be stuck in the pipeline. Sartre's failure to complete *Les Chemins de la Liberté* is unfortunate not only because it deprives his readers of the pleasure of finding out how it all officially ends. It is only in the light of what Mathieu finally achieves that we can understand why he should be so critically treated in the first volumes, and the lack of an ending consequently leaves a quite unnecessary ambiguity.

Sartre's interest in techniques of narration, which gives unity to the essays in *Situations I*, also recurs in the construction of each volume in *Les Chemins de la Liberté*. In *L'Age de Raison*, for example, each section of the novel describes how the events appear to one individual, and Sartre is very careful not to adopt the attitude of God-like omniscience which he found so annoying in Mauriac. In *Le Sursis*, he deliberately imitates the technique of 'simultaneity' developed by John Dos Passos in *Manhattan Transfer* and the *USA Trilogy*, and evokes the atmosphere of world-wide terror which characterized the Munich crisis by moving very rapidly, sometimes on the same page, from place to place and from one set of people to another.

This is very effective, and *Le Sursis* can be re-read with profit during any international crisis. Moreover, Sartre's technique also has important philosophical connotations, which again show how fruitful it is to study the whole of his work in the light of his remark that the existentialism which he represents is an attempt to think out all the consequences of a consistent atheism. On the train which is taking him to join his regiment in Paris, Mathieu thinks about the problem of presenting a complete picture of the modern world.

> If you tried to look directly at the planet, it would disintegrate into tiny fragments, and nothing but consciousnesses would be left. A hundred million free consciousnesses, each aware of a wall, a glowing cigar butt, familiar faces, and each of which constructed its destiny on its own responsibility. And yet, if one were one of these consciousnesses, one would realize, by imperceptible contacts and insensible changes, that one was a cell in an immense but invisible coral growth. War: everyone is free, and yet the chips are already down. The war is there, everywhere, it makes up the whole of my thoughts, the whole of Hitler's words, the whole of Gomez's acts; but no one is there to add it all up. The war exists only for God. But God does not exist. And yet the war exists.[33]

It is impossible to write a novel from the point of view of God, for God is dead, and the coherence which could have come from looking at things from his point of view is unattainable. All that the novelist can do is to present the individual minds which are conscious of the all-pervading war and reproduce the confusion of a world where God is dead. In the description of the reactions

of these minds, it can be shown that man is always controlled by
the circumstances of his life, and is yet free to adopt whatever
attitude he pleases towards them.

The only sections which have appeared of the projected
fourth volume, *La Dernière Chance*, are two extracts entitled
'Drôle d'Amitié', published in *Les Temps Modernes* in November
and December 1949. Brunet, the Communist, keeps up the morale
of his fellow-prisoners of war by telling them that the USSR will
soon be joining into the war against Germany, but is interrupted
when a senior comrade, Chalais, arrives at his Stalag. He soon
tells Brunet that he has been following completely the wrong line,
and proceeds to destroy the hopes, confidence and political
enthusiasm which Brunet had earlier created. Moreover, he tells
him that Schneider, the friend he had made during his early
days of captivity, is none other than Vicarios, a sometime member
of the Communist Party excluded in September 1939 for his
opposition to the Nazi-Soviet pact.

Chalais so excites some of Brunet's ex-admirers against
Vicarios that they try to beat him up, and he is saved only by
Brunet's intervention. The two men decide to escape, but are
caught in the glare of a searchlight just as they have cut their way
through the barbed wire. Someone has obviously told the Germans,
and only Chalais's men were in the know. It is clear from
Schneider's real name that Sartre regards him as the innocent
scapegoat for the betrayal of the French working class by the
Communist Party between August 1939 and June 1941. It is,
moreover, thoroughly in keeping with Orestes's remark about
human life beginning on the far side of despair[24] that Brunet
should have to go through this experience before he attains the
authenticity promised to him in the unpublished continuation of
the novel, but rather ironic that he should do so through the loss
of a friendship which is described with more sympathy than any
other relationship in *Les Chemins de la Liberté*. Just as Sartre
begins to realize that there may be more to human relationships
than the inevitable conflicts described in *L'Etre et le Néant*, he
gives up writing novels.

6 Plays, politics and villains

i

The production of *Les Mains Sales,* on 2 April 1948, at the fashionable right bank Théâtre Antoine, brought Sartre more hostility from the French Communist Party than any other action he has ever performed. He was accused in *L'Humanité* of writing as a vulgar penny-a-liner in order to pander to the anti-Communism of the bourgeoisie, and in 1951, when the play was made into a film, some of the cinemas where it was shown had to have police-protection against specially organized Communist protests.[1] Sartre himself denies that *Les Mains Sales* was intended to be a criticism of the Communist party, but the fact that he has consistently refused, since 1952, to allow the play to be performed in the West, arguing that it can only intensify the Cold War, suggests that he may indeed feel a little guilty at the interpretation which can be placed upon it. In December 1948 the Soviet authorities tried to prevent the performance of *Les Mains Sales* in Helsinki as 'propaganda hostile to the USSR', and in thus carrying out their wishes, Sartre is implicitly admitting that the play does have what a Marxist would call an 'objective' meaning which he had not originally intended.[2]

Sartre declared in 1964, after the play had been performed in a slightly altered form in Hungary, that a possible source lay in the French political history of the 1930s.[3] Jacques Doriot had wanted the Communist party to form an alliance with the *Section Française de l'Internationale Ouvrière*, and had been excluded for deviation. A year later the Communist party did exactly what he suggested, though without acknowledging his original initiative. The audience who saw *Les Mains Sales* in 1948, however, were inevitably reminded of some more recent and better-known examples of how political parties try to secure tactical advantages by suddenly changing and even reversing their policy. Between 1939 and 1941, Communist parties all over the world had been required to change their foreign policy at least twice, dropping their hostility to Nazi Germany when the Molotov-Ribbentrop pact was signed in August 1939, and revising their view equally abruptly when Germany invaded Russia less than two years later. The Moscow state trials of the 1930s had also shown how the most loyal Communists could be suddenly revealed, overnight, as traitors in the pay of foreign imperialism, and similar events were taking place in Eastern Europe at the very time when Sartre's play was enjoying its ong and successful run. Like the *Réflexions sur la Question Juive, Les Mains Sales* dealt with a problem that was to the forefront of everybody's mind, and the only way in which it did not fulfil the requirements of *Qu'est-ce que la Littérature?* was in the support which it apparently gave to those who had little sympathy for socialist revolutions.

Sartre's unfamiliarity with English literature always creates something of a problem for readers of *Les Mains Sales*, since he sets the action for this violent political drama in an imaginary Eastern European country called Illyria. A young and idealistic member of the Proletarian party, Hugo Barine, accepts in March 1943 the mission of going as secretary to one of the party chiefs, Hoederer, in order to murder him. Hoederer has decided, for motives with which Hugo's immediate superior Louis violently disagrees, to effect a temporary alliance between the Proletarian party and two other resistance groups. He knows that liberation is imminent, for the Russians have defeated von Paulus at Stalingrad and are driving the Germans west. But he is afraid that if the small Proletarian party is set up by the Russians as the sole government of the country, it will have to bear the brunt of all the unpopularity for the rigorous measures which will be necessary after the war. If, on the other hand, it governs as part of an official alliance with the Pentagone and the nationalists, it will be able to lay the blame on its two partners. And since the real power will be exercised not by the government but by a clandestine committee in which the Proletarian party will have half the votes, the way will soon be open for it to take control of the whole country when the other parties have been discredited. It will avoid being known as the 'Russian party', and will escape the odium of having been imposed by an occupying army.

When Hugo accepts the job of killing Hoederer, he is not aware of all the arguments that can be put forward to justify this policy. He had joined the Proletarian party in a mood of violent rebellion against the middle class into which he was born, and is only too ready to accept Louis's suggestion that anyone who proposes to compromise the party's principles by an alliance with its two traditional enemies deserves to be shot. He is also anxious to prove himself as a man by taking part in direct action instead of merely preparing the party newspaper, but soon discovers that it is not easy to kill a man like Hoederer in cold blood. He gradually becomes fonder of Hoederer, and is about to change sides and accept his offer of help when an accident intervenes. He finds his wife Jessica in Hoederer's arms. Anger enables him to do what political conviction had been unable to inspire, and he shoots Hoederer. Hugo is imprisoned. After two years, however, he is released for good conduct, and comes to his girl friend Olga's flat. The main action of the play consists of a long flashback in which he tells her the story of how he killed Hoederer, and she expresses great relief at learning that he does not, even now, really know why he did it.

Shortly after 1943, she explains, orders arrived from Moscow to collaborate with the two other parties, and on terms which Hugo immediately recognizes as Hoederer's own. On thus learning that he did, in fact, kill Hoederer for nothing, Hugo refuses Olga's offer that he should forget everything that has happened and stay in the party under a different name. A man like Hoederer, he declares, does not die by accident, killed for a woman. He dies for his ideas and for his policies. By going out and getting himself killed by the party gunmen who he knows are waiting to shoot him down as a traitor and an awkward witness, Hugo declares that he will really be killing Hoederer. This time, however, it will be for motives which he is certain are the right ones.

It is by no means necessary, if one is to interpret *Les Mains Sales* as an attack on Communist politics, to regard Hugo as the hero of the play. He is a much less attractive character than Hoederer, and has joined the Proletarian party for motives that are almost entirely selfish. A man who had really understood what Hoederer stood for would have agreed to change his name and would have stayed in the party in the hope that he could still be useful, and it is certainly not Hoederer's concept of politics as the science of the possible that Hugo defends by protesting in the way he does against unscrupulous changes in the party line. Another title which Sartre considered giving to his play was *Les Biens de ce Monde*, and this would, had he finally chosen it, have emphasized the paucity of Hugo's claim to represent right action in politics. The 'goods of this world' enjoyed by members of the middle class include an idealistic approach to politics which is diametrically opposed to Hoederer's readiness to dirty his hands by accepting all and every means to put his policies into action.

It is only when one looks at what happens to Hoederer that *Les Mains Sales* becomes an indictment of how the Communist party destroys the very people who make the greatest efforts to serve it. In 1943, Louis's conviction that it is wrong to seek an alliance with the Pentagone is so intense that he arranges to have Hoederer killed for daring to propose it. Yet this conviction disappears in the twinkling of an eye when new orders are received from Moscow, and Louis's moral indignation is immediately turned against Hugo, his erstwhile ally and cat's paw. By that time, however, the harm has been done, and Hoederer is dead. What *Les Mains Sales* brings out, in this respect, is not only the ruthlessness but the wasteful futility of the way Communists behave. There is no doubt that Hoederer is a much more intelligent politician than Louis, just as Vicarios, in *Drôle d'Amitié*, is a better man than Chalais. He has, moreover, the great merit of being prepared to take the initiative on his own account, and to run risks in order to do what he thinks is right. Yet just as Chalais, the 'voice of the historical process'[4] is still alive after Vicarios has been killed, so Louis is still there at the end of *Les Mains Sales*, the eternal bureaucrat, subservient to whatever new and contradictory orders may arrive, the living explanation for the inability which Communism has shown in any of the Eastern European countries symbolized by Illyria – Hungary, Czechoslovakia, East Germany – to survive without the aid of the Red Army whose presence Hoederer so dreaded. The death of Hoederer, killed and betrayed in strict accordance with his own principles, is tragic. But it is a tragedy created by a flaw in the very heart of Communist doctrine and practice, the belief that the party line is, at one and the same time, sacred enough to authorize murder and sufficiently flexible to be changed at a moment's notice.

When *Les Mains Sales* was put on in New York, Sartre himself was moved to protest against the liberties which had been taken with his text. Although the term 'red gloves' is used in the play itself to describe Hugo's aristocratic readiness to kill people, it was asking for trouble to produce the play under that title in America in 1948. Other, less obviously political changes were made, as when Jessica's comment that Hoederer was vulgar became: 'He looks like a king'. Charles Boyer was playing the part in the Broadway production, and he apparently objected to too literal a translation. Partly because of changes of this type, but also because Hugo was presented as a mild, horn-rimmed spectacled young man with a minor job in the New Deal, the play was not so successful in New York as it was in Paris and London, and Sartre's refusal to allow further productions in the West has not given it a second chance.[5] In Paris, it had the longest run of all his plays and was performed to packed houses from April 1948 to September 1949. An ingenious journalist in *L'Aurore* once calculated that Sartre's royalties for that year came to some 40 million old francs (about fifty thousand pounds in modern English currency), with at least thirty-five thousand francs for every performance of *Les Mains Sales*. With figures like these being bandied about, and with the memory of how people coming to the first night were 'strongly recommended' to wear evening dress, it is perhaps not surprising that Sartre was accused of having sold out to the bourgeoisie. Almost without exception, right-wing critics like Thierry Maulnier welcomed the play as a masterpiece, whereas the further left one went, the more critical the reception became.[6]

Les Mains Sales is not, however, solely a political play. In the same way that it would be wrong to interpret it as a wholly deliberate attack on the Communist party, so it would be misleading to neglect the way Hugo's final situation expresses many of Sartre's earlier philosophical ideas on the relationship between what we do and what we are. When Hugo sets out to kill Hoederer, he imagines that such an act will confer upon him for ever the status of a Murderer. The creation of a 'transcendental ego' of this kind will, he hopes, enable him to escape from the perpetual doubts that he has about his own motives and personality, and in his readiness to accept everything that Louis tells him as the absolute truth about politics, he shows something of the same fear of freedom which made Lucien Fleurier adopt the ready-made values of fascism. His desire to commit an action that will define him for all time backfires in his face when he discovers, at the end of the play, that he is still free to give whatever interpretation he pleases to his killing of Hoederer. If he tells Olga that he is 'fit for salvage' and prepared to work for the party again, he will have committed a *crime passionnel* – a title which Sartre himself thought of giving to the play, and which is now that of its English translation.[7] If, on the other hand, he refuses to accept the new changes in the party line, his act becomes a political one by the attitude which he thus adopts towards it, and the 'boundary situation' in which he finds himself is a perfect illustration of Sartre's argument, in *L'Etre et le Néant*, that the meaning of the past always depends upon the projects which I have for the future.[8] Yet although Hugo enjoys the same freedom as Oreste to act and create values by his action, his political situation is quite different. The only way in which he can make his values prevail is by killing himself, and just as Oreste's triumphant assertion of values reflected the hopes which inspired the Resistance movement, so Hugo's situation represents the dilemma in which the liberal, non-Communist left found itself in the France of 1948.

It is significant in this respect that the composition of *Les Mains Sales* should have virtually coincided with Sartre's first and only involvement in the creation of a new political grouping, the foundation of the *Rassemblement Démocratique Révolutionnaire* in March 1948. This movement tried to create a force which would destroy capitalism while still maintaining democratic liberties, and hoped to build a bridge between the proletariat and the more liberal fringes of the bourgeoisie. The RDR ran what was officially a bi-monthly newspaper, *La Gauche*, in which Camus and Sartre both published articles, but only thirteen numbers appeared between May 1948 and March 1949, when the whole enterprise fizzled out. The last number of *La Gauche* appealed for negotiations over Indochina, for opposition to the Marshall plan, and for a democratization of Algeria, and it is perhaps significant that the Indochinese war went on for another six years, that the Marshall plan remained unaffected, and that some form of democracy became possible in Algeria only after 1962. Sartre noted that the failure of the *Rassemblement Démocratique*

Révolutionnaire had given him a lesson in 'political realism',[9] and he has not again tried to add to the multiplicity of political groups in France.

It would clearly be wrong, from its date of composition alone, to look upon *Les Mains Sales* as a deliberate comment on the failure of the RDR, though the Hugo of *Red Gloves* would probably have felt quite at home in its ranks. What both the play and the failure of the movement do underline, however, is the contradictory situation in which left-wing intellectuals like Sartre found themselves in post-war France. Only the Communist party had working-class support, but it was subservient to Moscow. It taught an absurd, oversimplified deterministic materialism, which Sartre accused, in *Matérialisme et Révolution*, of 'stifling the revolutionary project', and showed an equal incompetence in its political tactics. For a man like Sartre, who had proclaimed in *Matérialisme et Révolution*: 'I know that man can be saved only by the liberation of the working class. I know it simply by looking at the facts, without needing to be a materialist',[10] the political situation in 1948 constituted an impasse. Nothing could be done without the Communists; and yet it was impossible to collaborate with them. Intentionally or not, *Les Mains Sales* expressed the atmosphere of this period, when the unity of the Resistance had disappeared and the non-Communist left had not yet discovered the unity of purpose which it was later to achieve in its fight against the Algerian war.

Although Sartre may well agree with *Paris-Match* in seeing *Le Diable et le Bon Dieu* as his best play,[11] *Les Mains Sales* is certainly his most exciting. Its long and successful run in 1948 and 1949 showed that, had Sartre not imposed his self-denying ordinance, it could have become as popular with the theatre audiences as *Huis Clos*, and it is a pity that the theories of *Qu'est-ce que la Littérature?* involve taking bananas off the market when they acquire an anti-revolutionary flavour. The excellence of *Les Mains Sales* lies partly in the constant tension, partly in its ambiguity, and partly in Sartre's exploration of the relationship between Hugo and Hoederer. The typically Sartrean theme of sequestration recurs both in the fact that Hugo, Jessica and Hoederer are isolated from the rest of the world in the villa where most of the action takes place, and in Hugo's inability to escape from Olga's room without being shot down by the party gunmen waiting in the street outside. In almost every scene where Hugo and Hoederer appear together, the audience knows that Hugo might bring himself to shoot, and this tension is constantly being heightened by new twists and turns of the plot. Hugo is very much a Hamlet-type character, and there is an especially interesting parallel in his ability to act only when a sudden onset of emotion gives him the opportunity of forgetting his intellectual hesitations.

There is also a very amusing echo of Hamlet's admiration for Horatio in a scene where Hugo envies the solidity and lack of imagination which, in his view, characterizes Hoederer's body-guard, Slick, and there is even a possibility here that Sartre is guying his own ideas on the *pour-soi* and the *en-soi*. Hugo is very much a *pour-soi*, and like most intellectuals occasionally envies the apparent certainty and total coincidence of self with self which seems to be the exclusive privilege of front-row forwards.

Hoederer is undoubtedly the most sympathetically drawn character in the whole of Sartre's work, and the only one to give direct expression to a liking for mankind. Moreover, he does use such typically Sartrean terms that it is difficult to believe he is not speaking for his creator: 'I love men for what they are', he tells Hugo, 'with all their dirty tricks and all their vices. I love their voices and their warm hands which take hold of things and their skin, the skin of the most naked animal, and their worried look and the desperate fight which each of them keeps up against death and anguish. For me, it matters that there should be a man more or less in the world.'[12] The relationship which develops between Hoederer and Hugo is built first of all upon a paradox. Hoederer suspects from the very beginning what Hugo is planning to do and yet decides to trust him, whereas Hugo is ostensibly acting for idealistic motives and yet is lying to Hoederer in everything he does and says. What gives the play its emotional density, however, is the fact that the roles which they gradually assume come to resemble those of father and son, and this is especially interesting in the light of the ideas on fatherhood which Sartre expresses both in *Les Mots* and *Les Séquestrés d'Altona*. There, the natural father is represented as a tyrant whose only interest in his son lies in the opportunity he provides for an exercise of authority, and there is no hint that a father might actually help his son. In joining the Proletarian party, Hugo has deliberately rejected his natural father but is not mature enough to stand on his own feet. He is unconsciously looking for a father substitute, and the readiness with which Hoederer adopts him suggests that his quest finds a strong answering echo. In view of Sartre's and Simone de Beauvoir's decision not to have any children,[13] the sympathy with which Sartre depicts this aspect of Hoederer's and Hugo's relationship might indicate a certain nostalgia for a human experience which it was by now rather late for him to think of undertaking. Both Sartre and Simone de Beauvoir are so critical about the way that they themselves were brought up that it would have been instructive for them to have shown us all how it ought to be done. It is nevertheless well within the ethos which Sartre absorbed from Charles Schweitzer that the father-son relationship depicted in his books should compensate us for the absence of a real life situation.

In one of the scenes in which he tries to discourage Jessica from becoming too interested in him, Hoederer remarks rather tartly that the cause of female emancipation has never held any great appeal for him. When one remembers Simone de Beauvoir's passionate analysis of the injustice of woman's lot in the two volumes of *Le Deuxième Sexe*, it is an odd remark for Sartre's favourite character to make.[14] It could be explained solely by its context in the play, and Hoederer's later comment that women believe blindly in their ideas because they receive them ready-made is equally relevant to the discussion which he is then having with Hugo. His comment could also, however, be taken as a reference to the way Simone de Beauvoir has tended to echo Sartre's views without having many original ideas of her own, and the period immediately preceding the creation of *Les Mains Sales* was rather a disturbed one in their relationship.

Simone de Beauvoir describes in *La Force des Choses* how she had a long and rather unhappy affair with the American novelist Nelson Algren, while Sartre himself was much preoccupied with a certain M., whom he had met in America in 1945.[15] From the moment they became lovers, early in the 1930s, Sartre and Simone de Beauvoir had agreed that they would have 'ancillary loves' with other people, but both M. and Nelson Algren seem from Simone de Beauvoir's own account to have threatened to become something more. While both *La Nausée* and *L'Etre et le Néant* bear the dedication *Au Castor* (Sartre's nickname for Simone de Beauvoir, because, like the beaver whose name hers resembles in English, she works very hard), *Qu'est-ce que la Littérature?* and *Les Mains Sales* are dedicated to 'Dolorès', a name which Simone de Beauvoir tells us is a synonym for M. We know nothing else about M. apart from the fact that Sartre's most commercially successful play was dedicated to her, and can only speculate as to whether his political development might have been different if he had stayed with her. But by 1948, the affair seems to have been over, and Simone de Beauvoir's autobiography contains no analysis of any other 'ancillary loves' which seriously threatened their unity. Even when, in 1953, she virtually set up house with Claude Lanzmann, a journalist and writer some thirteen years her junior, her relationship with Sartre does not really seem to have been affected. Lanzmann strongly approved of the increasingly left-wing bias which Sartre's political ideas were taking at the time.[16]

ii

When Sartre first met Jean Genet in May 1944, on the terrace of the Café de Flore, the two men struck up an immediate friendship. Genet was an illegitimate child, abandoned by his mother the moment he was born, and had spent most of his life from the age of fifteen, when not actually in a reformatory or prison, earning a precarious living as a thief and homosexual prostitute. In July 1946, *Les Temps Modernes* published an extract from his forthcoming *Journal du Voleur*, an autobiographical work which he later dedicated to Sartre and Simone de Beauvoir, and in 1947 Sartre dedicated his essay on Baudelaire to him as well as managing to secure the award of the Prix de la Pléiade for Genet's play *Les Bonnes*. In the innumerable conversations which they had together, Sartre encouraged Genet to do all the talking, and the long study of him known eventually as *Saint Genet, Comédien et Martyr* was based not only on Genet's novels and plays but also on what Sartre had learned privately of Genet's life and experiences. Long extracts of this essay first appeared in review form in *Les Temps Modernes* between July and December 1950 under the Anouilhesque title of *Saint Genet ou Le Bal des Voleurs*, but the book itself did not appear until June 1952. It was then published, rather oddly, as the first volume of Genet's *Oeuvres Complètes*, but was not Sartre's only contribution to Genet's career. In July 1948, he had collaborated with Jean Cocteau in sending a joint letter to the President of the Republic appealing against the life sentence which had just been passed on Genet for a crime which he had not in fact committed, but which he had assumed on his own account in order to preserve the honour of his friend Jean Decarnin, killed on the barricades at the liberation of Paris. Genet received a free pardon, and has continued since to defy society solely by the literary work to which Sartre declared in 1948 that he was now wholly devoted.[17]

Saint Genet, Comédien et Martyr has been seen as an exceptionally successful application of the new methods of analysis which can be derived from a combination of Marxism, psychoanalysis and phenomenology.[18] It does indeed have strong Marxist overtones, both in its hostility to established middle-class society and in its insistence on the social predestination which made it virtually inevitable that Genet, an orphan born in 1910 and placed as a foster child with a peasant family in 1917, should have become a criminal. Originally, in Sartre's view, Genet would have been quite happy to be integrated into the peasant society where his foster parents lived. But because it was a society in which people were defined exclusively in terms of the land which they inherited, he had no chance of ever being accepted. He tried to integrate himself by stealing, but was caught. He was then, in the eyes of all the people who knew him, officially labelled as a thief, and it was this experience which, for Sartre, constituted the crisis in his childhood. Instead of trying to escape from this judgment, Genet decided deliberately to be for himself what he had become only by accident and in the eyes of other people;

and Sartre greatly admires him for having chosen himself within
his situation, acting like the authentic Jew who transforms his
status as 'a man whom other men think is a Jew'[19] into the
foundation for his personality and values. In Genet's case,
however, there was one important difference: he had no alternative
set of values to fall back on.

What causes Vicarios, in *Drôle d'Amitié*, the most acute
suffering is that the standards of the Communist party, according
to which he is now a traitor, are an integral part of his own
personality. This experience of being haunted and inhabited by
one's fiercest judge is central to Sartre's analysis of Genet.
Even in his worst excesses, writes Sartre, he never casts off the
'simple-minded, theological morality'[20] of the small landowners
who had taken him into their home just as he had reached the
crucial phase in his childhood development, and in this respect
Genet's defiance of established standards, both in his life and
work, is curiously similar to the attempts made by life-long
Communists who have left the party to shake off the values it has
inculcated into them. What Genet's work shows us, claims
Sartre, is that morality nowadays is both 'inevitable and
impossible',[21] and this remark can easily be taken in a political
context: we have to pursue our revolutionary project, but can
never achieve success because the historical moment when our
action could be effective has not yet arrived. In his political
essays, Sartre comes back repeatedly to the idea that we are
living at a time when, as he says in *Saint Genet, Comédien
et Martyr*, 'we are never sure that we shall not retrospectively
become traitors',[22] and much of the fascination which Genet's
moral dilemma exercised over Sartre undoubtedly stemmed from
the wholly involuntary expression which his novels gave to
Sartre's own feelings about the political situation of the left-wing
sympathizer who either had been a member of the Communist
party or who had been tempted to join and had never succeeded
in doing so.

These chance political similarities are not, however, the only
explanation for Sartre's interest in Genet. In Sartre's view,
Genet's decision to be a thief did not merely mean the conscious
adoption of a life of ordinary crime. 'This little pilferer', he writes,
'longs for the moment when he will be entirely possessed and torn
apart by the terrible essence of the Evil-Doer',[23] and he provides
a very detailed description of the various attempts which Genet
made to achieve the absolute evil which alone could satisfy
this essentially metaphysical ambition. The betrayal of his fellow
criminals to the police is the worst action Genet can think of
performing, and yet even this, he comes to realize, eventually
serves the cause of the Good: the more criminals the police
capture, the stronger society becomes. Genet's failure to achieve

absolute evil in real life is closely connected with the play
that Sartre wrote immediately after *Saint Genet, Comédien et
Martyr, Le Diable et le Bon Dieu,* for here again the central theme
is that man can achieve neither absolute evil nor absolute good.
Indeed, Goetz's realization that his violence and treason serve only
the interest of the rich corresponds exactly to the disillusion
which Sartre describes Genet as feeling for his isolated and
anarchistic revolt. Genet does, however, triumph over society
in a way that is very different from the one which Goetz seems
likely to achieve when, at the end of the play, he agrees to take
command of the rebel army. Genet's novels, claims Sartre,
affect the middle-class reader by making him realize, through the
imaginative effort which he has to make to understand them,
that all the crimes and perversions which Genet describes are an
integral part of his own latent personality. 'Homosexual through
the power of words,' writes Sartre, 'we taste for a moment, in
the realm of the imaginary, the forbidden pleasure of taking a
man and being taken, and we cannot taste it without horrifying
ourselves.' Novels such as *Notre-Dame-des-Fleurs* or *Miracle de la
Rose* are, he writes, like the sleeping serpent which the peasant
placed in his own bosom in order to warm it back to life: the
moment they come alive, they sting.

iii

Another resemblance between *Saint Genet, Comédien et Martyr*
and *Le Diable et le Bon Dieu* lies in the fact that both contain
an appeal to revolution. This is perhaps only implicit in the study
of Genet, where Sartre's description of him as 'one of the
innumerable victims of our abject society'[25] is paralleled by a long
analysis of our present political impotence, but quite open in
Le Diable et le Bon Dieu, where the central character leaves the
stage, at the end of the play, with the same determination to
lead a peasant army which Bariona had shown in 1940. The
works are also similar in that they both contain an analysis and
rejection of the idea of religion, and especially of sainthood. In
Saint Genet, Comédien et Martyr, this concentrates on Genet's
attempt to become a saint by undergoing all possible forms of
humiliation, and leads at one point to what is perhaps the most
surprising *non sequitur* in modern literature: 'For my part, I like
human excrement less than people say, and that is why I refuse
sanctity wherever it manifests itself, in canonized saints as well
as in Genet.'[26] In *Le Diable et le Bon Dieu* it takes a more easily
understandable form. Goetz, who fails when he tries to achieve
absolute evil, decides on the flip of a coin that he will change
sides completely and devote himself to realizing absolute good.
He gives up being a professional soldier who betrays his own

brother and kills as much for pleasure as for profit, and founds
his own 'City of the Sun' where all men will devote themselves
to love and harmony. But Goetz discovers that good, in the
atmosphere of permanent civil strife which characterizes early
sixteeenth-century Germany, has even more disastrous results
than evil. He exercises true Christian charity in giving all his
lands to the poor, but this sets off a premature rebellion in the
rest of Germany. When this revolt fails, and the peasant army
seems about to be annihilated, Goetz realizes that isolated
individual attempts to improve man's lot are doomed to failure.
His final 'rejection of the absolute' comes when he goes back to
soldiering and accepts command of the peasant army, placing
himself at the service of Nasty, the revolutionary leader whose
ideas he had earlier spurned. One of the soldiers refuses to obey
an order, and Goetz stabs him to death. Like Hoederer, he accepts
that all means are good which serve the cause of revolution, and
abandons his Hugo-like attempt to change the world while refusing
to get his hands dirty.

For Simone de Beauvoir and Francis Jeanson, Goetz is an
infinitely preferable hero to Orestes. He chooses to stay with those
he is going to liberate, and this exemplifies the view which Sartre
himself formulated in 1965 when he said that the struggle for
liberation had to be fought and won every day.[27] Sartre also
remarked that he made Goetz do what he was incapable of doing
himself,[28] and there do seem to be some very close links between
the way Goetz solves his problems and Sartre's own realization,
in the years leading up to the publication of Les Mots, that he
had been totally misunderstanding the function of literature
by regarding it as a means of perpetuating spiritual values.
Originally, he thought that the writer could stand above and apart
from the struggles of other men, just as Goetz had stood aside in
the early stages of the peasants' rising and concentrated on his
own relationship with God. However, as Sartre completes what
he calls in Les Mots the 'cruel, long-drawn out enterprise' of
atheism, he comes to realize that, like Goetz, he must be 'a man
among men', 'anyone at all', and give up the superior status
enjoyed by a Roquentin or an Orestes.[29]

This interpretation of Le Diable et le Bon Dieu in the biographical framework of Les Mots is naturally open to the objection that
it takes for granted a view of Sartre's literary career which is
totally contradicted by every book he has ever published. After
the Sartre of Qu'est-ce que la Littérature? has openly stripped
authorship of its semi-sacred status, it is superfluous for Goetz
to do the same thing through what has been seen by some critics
as a rather laboured allegory. Where the biographical relevance
of Le Diable et le Bon Dieu is less in dispute is in the similarity
between Goetz's final action and the political attitudes which

Sartre adopted in the early 1950s. The play was produced at the *Théâtre Antoine* on 7 June 1951 and almost exactly one year later Sartre committed himself firmly to supporting the Communist party, 'on the basis of my principles, not theirs', in the first of the articles entitled *Les Communistes et la Paix*.[30] In August 1952, he publicly quarrelled with Albert Camus, arguing that one acquired the right to criticize a political movement only by taking part in it oneself, not by standing on the side-lines and trying to be an impartial spectator.[31] This is very much in the spirit of Goetz's final resolution, and Sartre's presence, in December of the same year, as a speaker at the Communist inspired World Peace Conference in Vienna left no doubt as to where his sympathies lay. Admittedly, he never became a Goetz-type leader, and his formal insistence on the need for the left to 'answer violence by violence' did not come until ten years after the first performance of *Le Diable et le Bon Dieu*. Nevertheless, his influence on young French intellectuals was greater in the early 1950s than at any other time in his career, and in that sense he was an acknowledged leader in the relatively narrow political world open to him.

Le Diable et le Bon Dieu belongs to that class of Sartre's works which are more remarkable for their complexity than their concision. Even after he had agreed to make the most drastic cuts, the play still ran for over four hours, and the directors of the *Théâtre Antoine* had to take the unprecedented step of requiring the audience to be in place before eight o'clock. Again like *Saint Genet, Comédien et Martyr*, *Le Diable et le Bon Dieu* is rich in apparent irrelevancies, and at the furthest possible remove from those other works by Sartre which, like *Huis Clos* or *Les Mains Sales*, have an almost classical simplicity of line. By what is perhaps more than just a coincidence, it is Sartre's longer and more complex works which have the most marked left-wing political implications, and in this respect *La Critique de la Raison Dialectique* follows the same pattern as *Saint Genet, Comédien et Martyr* or *Le Diable et le Bon Dieu*. Sartre once said that he wrote for three hours every morning and three hours every afternoon,[32] and the length of some of his works bears this out. Even when, after 1952, his attitude towards politics seemed to change quite radically, it was still through the written word that he tried to act on the society of his time, and there is little of real significance that can be said about the actual life which he led. He gave up teaching in 1945, and has since devoted the whole of his time to writing. He keeps almost none of his large royalties for himself, but gives his money away to people or causes which arouse his sympathy. He has few possessions, and nothing which could be called a 'home life'. Much of his time is spent in cafés, and in 1945 he published a curious exchange of

views with a Catholic priest called Roger Troisfontaines on this
very point. Troisfontaines had accused Sartre of drifting aimlessly
through life, with no normal contacts with his fellows, no friends,
no family and no centre to his existence. Sartre replied that he
did indeed spend his days in cafés, and it was there that he had
written all his books. He found them more congenial places to
work in than a home where his wife and children would 'tiptoe
around so as not to disturb him'. In a café, he said, he could
ignore the conversations taking place around him, could look up
when a pretty girl came in and then go back to his work, feeling
life going on around him without having to join in. When one
remembers how ghastly his early home life was in the Schweitzer
flat, it is not difficult to understand why he should refuse
conventional middle-class standards just as vigorously in his
private life as he does in his books, and it is again a point of
resemblance between him and Genet that neither of the two men
has either a home or any other possessions. Sartre, apparently,
even goes to the extent of not owning any books.[33]

Where Sartre does enjoy what most people would regard as a
high standard of living is in the amount of time he spends
travelling abroad. In the 1930s he and Simone de Beauvoir
visited almost every country in Europe, and they kept up this
habit after the war. After his trip to America late in 1945, he went
to Holland in 1946, Sweden and Lapland in 1947, Germany in
1948 – giving a lecture in Berlin to mark the first performance
outside France of *Les Mouches* – to Algeria in 1948, to South
America in 1949 – stopping at Havana to call on Hemingway,
who had called Sartre a general and himself a captain when they
met in Paris in 1945[34] – Black Africa in 1950, and to Norway,
Iceland and Scotland in 1951. What Simone de Beauvoir calls
'Scottish austerity' made a poor impression on them when they
had to catch a boat at ten o'clock one morning. They found no
café or restaurant prepared to serve them tea or coffee or even let
them shelter from the pouring rain. They were happier in Italy,
where Sartre has spent almost every summer since 1952. The
Italian Communist Party followed a more independent line than
the French, and its leaders and intellectuals were consequently
more sympathetic to Sartre's point of view. After the outbreak
of the Algerian war in November 1954, explains Simone de
Beauvoir, there were also other reasons why both she and Sartre
felt more at home in Italy. In a country which had lost all its
colonies in 1945, the people they met in the street were not, as
they were in France, 'accomplices in massacres and tortures'[35].
In 1953, Sartre and Simone de Beauvoir visited Tunisia, at that
time still a French protectorate struggling to obtain its
independence. When a young Tunisian docker saw that Sartre's
motor car was having to wait for a long time before being loaded

on to a boat, he called to his friends to help him straight away. Simone de Beauvoir remarks how she felt a twinge of envy at Sartre's ability to bring 'laughter and friendship into faces which France had condemned to hatred',[36] and the incident perhaps epitomizes the relationship which Sartre established, in the 1950s and 1960s, with the colonial nations striving to attain their independence. Together with the attempt to liberalize Communism, it is the struggle against European colonialism which has occupied most of Sartre's energy over the last eighteen years, changing him from an author with a keen interest in politics into a virtually full-time political writer.

Part III

Communism, plays and Hungary

i

In the long essay which he wrote in 1961 to pay tribute to his
life-long friend and erstwhile political ally, Maurice Merleau-
Ponty, Sartre explained in some detail how he had come to adopt
the political attitude which, in 1955, had led to a quarrel between
the two men.[1] The crucial event was the invasion, on 25 June
1950, of South Korea by troops from the Communist-dominated
North. Merleau-Ponty, reacting against the sympathy for
Communism which had made him seem, in the years immediately
after World War II, even further to the left than Sartre himself,
saw in this invasion the definitive proof that Stalinism had
become an aggressive 'Bonapartiste' militarism. By a curious re-
versal of the normal relationship between an editor and his review,
Sartre was led to adopt quite a different attitude in and by *Les
Temps Modernes*. I. F. Stone and E-N. Dzenepely sent in articles
showing the outbreak of the war in a new light, and it was on the
basis of the information which they contained that Sartre accepted
the version of events which he now holds: that General MacArthur
and President Syngman Rhee were both determined that a war
should break out, the first because he wanted to crush Communist
China, the second because he aimed at annexing the industries
of North Korea; that if the North Korean troops attacked first,
it was after a series of provocative frontier incidents; and that the
whole operation was a trap which the American militarists and
their feudal allies had laid for the Chinese.[2]

To read 'Merleau-Ponty vivant', published as a preface to the
special number which *Les Temps Modernes* devoted in October
1961 to discussing Merleau-Ponty's work and ideas, is to
understand something of the real political conflicts exercising
Sartre's mind when he was writing *Le Diable et le Bon Dieu*.
His conviction that the aggressor in the Cold War was the United
States and not the Soviet Union had already been implicit in the
choice of articles published in *Les Temps Modernes* in the late
1940s, attacking the Marshall Plan as an imperialist manoeuvre
while saying nothing about the Russian attempt to seize control
of West Berlin by blockading the city between 24 June 1948 and
12 May 1949, but did not come fully into the open until the
appearance of the first part of *Les Communistes et La Paix* in July
1952. 'However hard I look', writes Sartre in this article, 'I can
find over the last thirty years no aggressive ambitions on the part
of the Russians'.[3] Russian foreign policy, he argues, is dominated
by the fear of being encircled by an aggressive Western alliance

as well as by the memories of the hostility which greeted the
newly created socialist state after the revolution of 1917. In what
sometimes reads like an ironic echo of the attitude towards evil
which he attributes to the Just Man in *Saint Genet, Comédien et
Martyr,* he satirizes the western politicians and journalists who
have a totally Manichean view of history and see in Soviet
policy only an inexplicable but unyielding desire to cause harm.
Far better, he suggests, examine our own conduct and see if it
is not rather the hostility which the West has shown towards
Communism that has created its own mirror image in the
apparently aggressive behaviour of the Soviet Union. Such a
self-examination, he maintains, will be even more appropriate as
we become more conscious of the violence which capitalist society
has always shown towards its own working class. If the
Communist party receives, as it did in 1952, the support of the
French proletariat, it is because this class recognizes that the
Communist party represents its interests. This is the idea which
Sartre pursues throughout the three long articles entitled *Les
Communistes et La Paix.*

Simone de Beauvoir describes Sartre as having been greatly
impressed, in 1952, by the French historian Henri Guillemin's
study of how Napoleon III seized power in France by the
military *coup d'état* of 2 December 1851. In his youth, she said,
impressed by the genuine qualities of his stepfather, Sartre had
refused to agree with his Communist friends in seeing the
bourgeoisie as incapable of possessing any virtues. Among
themselves, he would argue, they could act with some generosity,
and the fact that M. Mancy had sympathized with the Gaullist
resistance movement during the war suggested to him that
they could act with occasional political integrity as well. But
Guillemin's book showed Sartre to what violence and ruthlessness
men as apparently honest as his stepfather could descend when a
military adventurer offered to defend their interests.[4] Moreover, a
number of events which took place at the end of May and
beginning of June 1952 convinced Sartre that the French
bourgeoisie was preparing to treat the Communist party exactly
as the capitalists who supported Napoleon III had treated the
nineteenth-century working class. They wanted to kill off or
imprison the working-class leaders, and destroy the political
organizations which the workers were trying to form. 'In the name
of the principles which it had inculcated into me', wrote Sartre,
looking back in 1961 on how he had felt in the early summer of
1952, 'in the name of its humanism and "humane studies", in the
name of liberty, equality and fraternity, I swore against the
bourgeoisie a hatred which will finish only with my death'.[5] The
combination between his gradual realization of who was really
responsible for the outbreak of the Korean war, his reading of

Guillemin's *Le Coup d'Etat du 2 Décembre,* and his interpretation
of what was actually happening in France, brought Sartre to the
point where he could do in fact what Goetz had done only on the
stage: ally himself with the political force which seemed to him,
at the time, to be most threatened by the class in power and
keenest to overthrow an unjust social system.

The immediate events which led to this crystallization of
Sartre's political attitude began when the French Communist
Party tried to organize a demonstration, on 28 May 1952, to
protest against the arrival in Paris of General Ridgway, General
Eisenhower's successor as head of SHAPE. In spite of the fact that
the Communist press had for months been denouncing General
Ridgway as responsible for using germ warfare in Korea, the
demonstration was a complete failure. Nevertheless, the French
government arrested the secretary of the Communist party,
Jacques Duclos, and accused him of having intended to use the
two dead pigeons found in the back of his car to carry the news
of the street fighting back to Moscow. The editor of *L'Humanité,*
André Stil, had already been arrested for incitement to riot, and
it seemed both to Sartre and to the Communist party itself that
the government was preparing to outlaw it completely. It issued
an appeal for a general strike to take place on 4 June, but this was
an even greater flop than the demonstration. What aroused
Sartre's ire was not so much what he saw as the obvious
manoeuvres of the French government. It was the delight shown
by journalists of the non-Communist left at this spectacle of the
Communist party's failure to make the workers do what it wanted.
Indeed, it was to protest against the view that the French working
class had now officially disowned the Communist party and all its
works that he wrote, in an access of fury which kept him up for a
day and a night, the first part of *Les Communistes et la Paix.*
'One cannot fight the working class without becoming an enemy
of mankind and of oneself', he declared, and since the Communist
party was the only party in France to represent the working class,
it followed that the journalists who rejoiced in its discomfiture
were going against the only hope of avoiding war and restoring both
the prosperity and the national independence of France. In
Sartre's view, every time a modern factory owner talked –
as Monsieur Fleurier talks in *L'Enfance d'un Chef* – of the 'common interests of workers and capitalists', his workers saw him
as the descendant of those who had massacred their forefathers
in June 1848 and of those involved in the repression of the
Commune in May 1871.[6] In France, the class war was a reality,
and the only organization capable of rallying the workers
was the Communist party. Incidents such as the failure of the
demonstration and strike in May and June 1952 had no long-
term significance.

Sartre's articles in *Les Communistes et la Paix* had a considerable impact on a number of young Frenchman, not least in the Ecole Normale Supérieure de la rue d'Ulm. As he implicitly admits, however, such arguments have little relevance in countries such as the United States or Great Britain, where the Communist party has never enjoyed any significant working-class support. These articles are important in his own career, partly for the indication which they give of his readiness to exchange imaginative literature for what W. H. Auden calls the 'flat, ephemeral pamphlet',[7] and partly because of their relevance to his later ambition of renovating Marxism by grafting on to it some of the concern for immediate, lived events characteristic of existentialism. Their appearance coincided with other gestures of public support which he gave to international as well as to French Communism between 1952 and 1956. In the early summer of 1954, he visited Russia, and published a series of enthusiastic articles in the fellow-travelling newspaper *Libération*.[8] After spending two months in China, in autumn 1955, he declared that the masses were now genuinely determining their own fate.[9] In both 1953 and 1954, he spoke in Paris and Berlin at conferences organized by the Communist-dominated World Peace Congress, and in 1955 became vice-president of the Association France-URSS. What is perhaps more interesting, from both a literary and a biographical point of view, is that the two plays which he wrote and had performed during this period, *Kean* and *Nekrassov*, end in a similar way to *Bariona* and *Le Diable et le Bon Dieu*: in the final scene, the hero accepts a more coherent and disciplined attitude towards society.

ii

It might at first sight seem strange to consider Sartre's adaptation of the play *Kean ou Désordre et Génie,* supposedly by Alexandre Dumas *père*,[10] as in any way relevant to his political evolution. He wrote it at the request of Pierre Brasseur, who had played the part of Hoederer in the 1951 film adaptation of *Les Mains Sales* as well as that of Goetz in *Le Diable et le Bon Dieu*, and used it primarily as a vehicle for exploring a problem which had preoccupied him ever since he and Charles Schweitzer had so successfully incarnated the roles of affectionate grandson and devoted grandfather: that of the relationship between real and feigned emotions. Kean's paradox is that he is really himself only when playing a part, and the similarity with the café waiter in *L'Etre et le Néant* who can coincide with what he is only by playing at being a café waiter is fairly obvious. However, *Kean* also has a number of social and even autobiographical overtones which link it firmly to Sartre's later development.

Like Genet, the English actor – manager Edmund Kean was born outside wedlock, and at one point in the play virtually quotes a phrase from *Saint Genet, Comédien et Martyr* when he cries out to the audience: 'You have taken a child and transformed him into a monster'.[11] By regarding the first as a source of amusement and the second as the incarnation of wickedness, society has effectively prevented both Kean and Genet from developing any authentic personality of their own, and they are both semi-autobiographical figures on to whom Sartre has projected something of his own childhood situation and experiences. He too was regarded as an infant prodigy who could be relied upon to flatter the vision which the adults had of themselves, and when Kean announces his intention of leaving the Drury Lane theatre, where people only laugh at him if he stops being Othello and becomes really jealous on his own account, he could almost be describing how the infant Jean-Paul sought refuge in the epic world of his comics when reality refused to take him seriously.[12] In 1956, Kean's and Genet's bastardy was taken by Francis Jeanson, in his *Sartre par lui-même,* as the defining characteristic of the Sartrean hero, and while Sartre himself was reluctant to endorse this as a wholly accurate description of himself, he did acknowledge that the combination between his lack of a real father and the wholly unreliable affection of Charles Schweitzer gave him the status of a 'faux bâtard' which almost fitted Jeanson's analysis.[13] What is more important, however, both from a dramatic and a personal standpoint, is the conclusion which Sartre gives to *Kean.* Just as Goetz abandons his concern with the transcendent world of religion, Kean stops trying to be accepted by the aristocratic world of Regency England. He falls in love with a young girl called Anna Damby, and they both go off to America, where he will continue to be an actor but in a different more democratic society. Like Goetz, he settles for the immediate and relative tasks which lie within man's grasp, and here again becomes something of an autobiographical figure. By 1953, if Sartre's own dates for his development as a writer are to be believed, he too had begun to give up an absolutist concept of literature. He had certainly accepted the humbler task of writing articles on the practical question of what attitude people ought to have towards the Communist party, and like Bariona, Orestes and Goetz, Kean leaves the stage with the conviction of having at last found his true path. The replacement of his high-born mistress Elena, Countess of Koefeld, by plain Anna Damby can also be seen as a curious transformation into sexual terms of the greater modesty which Sartre claims to have adopted, in the early 1950s, towards his literary calling.

The play which immediately followed *Kean* was presented by Sartre himself as stemming from the promise which he had

taken at the Vienna Peace Conference of 1952 to make his
own contribution as a writer to the cause of world peace.[14]
Nekrassov, first produced at the Théâtre Antoine on 8 June 1955,
is a satire on the excesses in which the French anti-communist
press indulged in the early 1950s; and perhaps because it was
so hostile to journalists it had a remarkably bad reception
from the critics. It had the shortest run of any of Sartre's plays
– only eighty-eight performances – and Sartre and Simone de
Beauvoir were perhaps right in attributing this to the reluctance
of the French bourgeoisie to go and see a play which questioned
the widely-held view that all Communists were dangerous
villains plotting the destruction of Western values. It was certainly
better received when produced in a more neutral political
atmosphere at the Edinburgh festival in 1957, though it is a
paradox that such a highly committed play should be successful
only when the audience is not sufficiently concerned with what
it says to feel annoyed.

The play describes how a professional confidence trickster,
Georges de Valera, successfully pretends to be a well known
Russian politician called Nekrassov, who has 'chosen freedom'
and defected to the West. He is gladly adopted by a right-wing
newspaper, which badly needs anti-Communist propaganda to
help the government win an important by-election, and soon
becomes the idol of fashionable Paris. He invents the most
hair-raising stories about the horrors of Communism, but
discovers that his innocent pranks can have serious consequences
when two left-wing journalists whom he had accused of receiving
Russian gold are threatened with imprisonment. He sees the light,
and ends his joke in a politically laudable manner by giving an
exclusive interview to the left-wing paper, *Libérateur*, in which he
reveals what a hoax the whole thing has been.

The fact that de Valera – Sartre really does have a genius for
choosing the wrong name for the English ear – leaves the stage with
an attractive left-wing woman journalist called Véronique, the
daughter of the right-wing editor whom he has been fooling
throughout the play, also heightens the resemblance with the
ending of *Kean*. Like Goetz, de Valera abandons a purely
individualistic and anarchical revolt against society in favour of
what one can only assume will be a life of political commitment
by the side of a girl whom one French critic rather unkindly
described as a Joan of Arc of progressive politics.[15] This
combination of sexual and political optimism strikes a new note in
Sartre's work, and there is no doubt that he is writing, in
Nekrassov, from the point of view of someone genuinely convinced
that Russia wants peace in the normal sense of the word, and that
the only danger of war comes from the excesses of anti-Communism. This may have been true for a very short period in the

mid-1950s, but the satire in *Nekrassov* took on a very jaundiced appearance between 1957 and 1962, when scarcely a month went by without Mr. Krushchev threatening to blow us all up. Sartre was placed in an equally embarrassing position when the appearance of Krushchev's report to the Twentieth Party Congress in 1956 showed that a fair number of the accusations levelled against Stalinism by newspapers such as *Soir à Paris* had been substantially ·correct. However, this report also had other consequences which rather put *Nekrassov* in the shade, and which led to a serious break between Sartre and the Communist party.

iii

Stalin's death in March 1953 had been followed by a slow thaw in Russian home and foreign policy, and when Krushchev took the quite exceptional step of denouncing Stalin's crimes, there seemed to be a chance of freedom even for the peoples of Eastern Europe on whom Russia had imposed its rule after 1945. Poland was the first country to obtain some measure of independence when Gomulka came back to power in June 1956, and the dismissal in Hungary of the Stalinist dictator Rakosi, together with the return of Imre Nagy in October 1956, suggested that this country too might be able to adopt what was known at the time as 'national Communism'. However, once Nagy had tried to acquire some genuine independence by withdrawing from the Warsaw Pact, the Russians decided to intervene. On 4 November, the Red Army attacked and occupied Budapest, and the experiment with liberalism was over. In an interview published in *L'Express* on 9 November 1956, Sartre denounced this repression of the Hungarian revolt as a crime, and condemned it 'absolutely and without hesitation'. He added, however, that it had been made virtually inevitable by 'twelve years of terror and stupidity'; and it is his explanations of how this terror and stupidity originated which gave his criticism of Russian policy a different tone from the protests which many other writers and thinkers were making at the time. What the Russian intervention threatened, he argued, was the future of socialism itself, and it was socialism alone, not the bourgeois concepts of justice and international law, which had the right to condemn it.

Sartre's more detailed analysis and condemnation of the Russian action took the form of a long article entitled '*Le Fantôme de Staline*', which served in January 1957 as introduction to a special number which *Les Temps Modernes* devoted to the Hungarian rising. For the first thirty years or so after 1917, argued Sartre, the need to industrialize a very backward country had created a basic contradiction in early Soviet society between 'the interests of socialist construction and . . . the immediate interests of the working class'. Without the unifying personality of Stalin and the rigid control exercised by the party, such a contradiction would have made the building up of socialism impossible. Stalinism was thus, for Sartre, not a deviation from a true socialism which might perhaps have existed 'among Plato's Eternal Essences', but a 'detour imposed upon it by the force of circumstances'. Indeed, he writes, one had to choose between Stalinism with all its faults, 'this bloodstained monster which destroys itself', and no socialism at all.[16] Where, however, the Stalinists over-reached themselves was in their mistaken view that their form of socialism could be imposed upon the Eastern European countries liberated by the Red Army in 1944 and 1945.

In one sense Sartre regards this decision to export Stalinism as having been forced upon the Russians. What he calls the 'war-like manoeuvre'[17] of the Marshall Plan compelled them to impose a rigid control over their satellites in order to avoid the danger of Poland or Hungary becoming the advanced bastions of a future American crusade against Communism. Nevertheless, the Russians were also convinced that it was somehow good for all countries to follow the same difficult road to socialism which the USSR had had to take. Because the economic conditions of post-revolutionary Russia had prevented the Communist party leaders from ever trusting their own proletariat, they assumed that the working class in Eastern Europe would be equally hostile to the introduction of socialism. In this, argues Sartre, they were wrong. The motor industry installed in Poland may not have produced very good motor cars but it made excellent workers, and the great error which the Russians committed in Hungary in 1956 was not to trust the ability of the working class to defend socialism without the intervention of foreign troops. By its resistance to 'the strongest army in the world', the Hungarian working class had shown how well organized and determined it was. And had the Russian leaders been able to free themselves from Stalin's ghost, which alone made them prefer power politics to rational persuasion, the Hungarian revolution of 1956 would have produced its own socialist state.

Sartre's declaration, in November 1956, that he was 'firmly but reluctantly' breaking off contact with all Communist writers who did not denounce the Russian invasion of Hungary, and was resigning from the Association France–URSS, appeared at first sight to constitute a complete break with the policy he had been following since 1952. Moreover, several of the arguments and presuppositions of *Le Fantôme de Staline* show a remarkable continuity with the political views he had expressed in the late 1940s and early 1950s, the period at which he had been most hostile to Communism. The policy which Hoederer outlined to Hugo in *Les Mains Sales* was principally intended to spare

Illyria the kind of military occupation and imposition of Communism from the outside which had caused all the trouble in Hungary, and in 1950, the year in which *Les Temps Modernes* had denounced the use of slave labour camps in the Soviet Union, Sartre's preface to Louis Delmas's book *Le Communisme Jougoslave Depuis Tito* had put forward very much the same criticism of Stalinist bureaucracy that was to inform '*Le Fantôme de Staline*'.[18] Yet although Sartre's reaction to the events of November 1956 seemed to indicate that his support for Communism between the years 1952 and 1956 had ended, the essays which he published later in 1957 show that this was not really so. In our own day, he wrote in *Questions de Méthode*, Marxism is 'the seed-bed of each individual thought and the horizon of all our cultural activities'.[19] No philosophy can go beyond it, for the circumstances which originally gave rise to it have not yet been transcended. However, Marxism is suffering from a temporary failure to develop all its potentialities, and it is here that existentialism, which Sartre declares is parasitic upon Marxism, can contribute to helping it out of the slough into which it has fallen. In 1956, the French Communist Party had swung into line and supported Russian policy in Hungary. Disappointed in what practising Communists actually did, Sartre turned his attention to how real Marxists ought to think.

The peculiarity of existentialism, he argued in 1957, is that it has always insisted upon the uniqueness of each individual person and each particular historical event. It began with Kierkegaard's protest against the pretensions of the all-embracing system set up by Hegel, and since that day has not ceased to assert the rights of the individual in the face of any such attempt to assimilate him into a general philosophy. By analysing each individual event from a Marxist standpoint, but without conforming to the fixed categories of the official party philosophers, it can lead men towards a greater understanding of the time in which they live. *Questions de Méthode* itself published in *Les Temps Modernes* in September and October 1957, after having first appeared in Poland,[20] does not give any particularly up to date examples of how this might be done, since the only 'concrete analyses' which it contains deal with the events of the first French revolution and the childhood of Gustave Flaubert. In a way, however, both '*Les Communistes et la Paix*' and '*Le Fantôme de Staline*' already put into practice the aim of '*Questions de Méthode*'. Sartre summarizes this when he writes that both existentialism and Marxism 'seek the same object; but the second has reabsorbed man into a general idea while the first looks for him everywhere, at work, at home, in the street',[21] and the style of thinking which reaches its first tentative conclusions in the 755 pages of *La Critique de la Raison Dialectique* in 1960 undoubtedly begins with *'Les Communistes et la Paix'* in 1952. Thus Sartre's analysis of French trade unionism is translated word for word from the second part of this essay into the philosophical work which aims at 'existentializing Marxism'.[22]

Sartre declares, on the very first page of *La Critique de la Raison Dialectique,* his basic agreement with 'historical materialism', in the sense that he accepts as true Engels's statement that men 'make their own history, but in given circumstances which condition them'. However, he considers that classical Marxism is guilty of having laid insufficient stress upon two fundamental aspects of the human condition: the overriding importance of scarcity; and the phenomenon to which he gives the rather impressive name of the *'pratico-inerte',* the process whereby man's conscious actions give quite unintended consequences. Even Marx, in Sartre's view, did not give enough weight to the fact that there is never enough to go round. He consequently did not see that the real basis for the class war lay in man's immediate recognition of his fellows not as potential helpmates but as rivals for the inadequate food and shelter available. No society, maintains Sartre, has yet passed beyond the stage where all human relationships are governed by scarcity, for even an economy characterized by over-production suffers from it under the form of a shortage of actual or potential consumers. Yet this is not the only aspect of the human condition which makes Sartre's account of experience in *La Critique de la Raison Dialectique* as pessimistic as the analyses in *L'Etre et le Néant.* In his attempt to solve the problem of scarcity, he argues, man falls into even greater difficulties when his own creations turn against him, and he is on some occasions literally strangled by his own success.

The first and most immediately telling example which Sartre gives of the *pratico-inerte* concerns the Chinese peasants who, in order to clear their land for cultivation, cut down all the trees. They thus exposed themselves, far more efficiently than any invading army could ever have done, to the danger of recurrent flooding. Just as Sartre's insistence on scarcity is highly relevant in a world where two-thirds of the population are quite literally dying of hunger, so this analysis of the *pratico-inerte* strikes an immediate chord in a society acutely conscious of pollution and conservation problems. Modern consumer society is indeed overflowing with examples which show how 'the machine fashions man just as man fashions the machine',[23] and the Chinese peasants who unintentionally flooded their own land are forerunners of the motorists stuck in traffic jams on highways built for rapid access to the seaside. The concept of the *pratico-inerte* was not, however, inspired primarily by the successes of capitalism. It stemmed from Sartre's political preoccupations in the 1950s, and his philosophical account of how man is alienated by his own creations is most immediately applicable to his analysis of Stalinism.

When Stalin and his followers chose their ruthless solution for the economic and political problems of post-revolutionary Russia, they were not, in Sartre's view, acting immorally. Indeed, his analysis of human behaviour in *La Critique de la Raison Dialectique* is, in theory at any rate, ethically neutral, and his condemnation of the invasion of Hungary in November 1956 pointedly eschewed any appeal to a supposedly universal code of morality. Men act in response to the circumstances in which they are placed, and when the Russian leaders gave the order for their troops to march into Budapest, they were just as much the victims of a system which had helped them conquer in the past as the willing accomplices in the crimes to which this system was still giving birth. Like the cleared land which enabled the Chinese peasants to cultivate their crops, the military and bureaucratic dictatorship established by Stalin gave the Russian leaders a tool which they could use to establish their will on virtually any satellite country. But at the same time, the very efficiency of this tool created a framework from which they found it impossible to escape. As a good Marxist, Sartre sees the present stagnation of Communist philosophy as the direct result of a particular set of economic and political circumstances. So long as the structure of Communist society remains the same, the philosophy reflecting it will not develop. Nevertheless, by what seems to be a prolongation of his earlier insistence on freedom, Sartre's attempt to de-Stalinize the French Communist Party by writing political philosophy presupposes that ideas are not wholly the passive reflection of economic circumstances. By acting on the way men think, one can influence the course of political events; and his struggle to release Western Communist thought from the influence of the *pratico-inerte* created by Stalinist bureaucracy is an enterprise which assumes that practical politics cannot be dissociated from philosophical analysis. The colonialist structure created by Western imperialism in the nineteenth century had also given rise to a *pratico-inerte* just as deadly in its effects as the triumph of Stalinism, and one which Sartre found it possible to combat with a less neutral attitude to the moral issues it raised.

8 Colonialism, violence and tragedy

In what was almost Sartre's first publication, *La Légende de la Vérité*, there is an ironic passage which seems to foreshadow the systematic opposition which he has shown to Western colonialism since 1946. 'You say that the Africans suffer from colonization. But come now, if that were the case, they would rebel. Yet you can see them, every hour of the day, grave and tranquil. They are too uncouth to congratulate themselves in public for the protection accorded to them. But they say nothing, which amounts to the same thing.'[1] *Les Temps Modernes* had been running for less than six months when the Marxist philosopher Tran Duc Thao published his '*Indochine SOS*' in the February 1946 number. Sartre's review thus began its campaign – several months before the French Communist Party's – against the colonial policy whereby the French governments of the Fourth Republic attempted to retain possession of Indochina, a French dependency from 1887 until its occupation by the Japanese in 1940. In November 1946, in an article entitled 'Et Bourreaux et victimes', it called for immediate negotiations between the French government and what was then largely a nationalist movement, the Viet-Minh, and kept up the battle over the years with a number of articles criticizing French policy. Sartre's own part in this campaign was relatively limited, and it was not until the 1960s, when he became a leading figure in the international opposition to America's Vietnam policy, that Indochina occupied very much of his attention. He did, however, put his name to one book devoted almost wholly to the Indochinese war, *L'Affaire Henri Martin*, in 1953, and his experience in this context made him acutely aware of the difference between the way official French society treated him when he was acting as a literary man and the attitude it adopted when political questions were at stake. In 1948, he and Jean Cocteau had had little difficulty in persuading President Auriol to grant Jean Genet a free pardon for his crimes. In 1952, he had a much less sympathetic response when he submitted a comparable petition on behalf of Henri Martin, a young sailor sentenced to five years in prison for opposition to the Indochinese war. For Sartre, it was the beginning of a harsh apprenticeship in learning the limits of the writer's immediate power, and one which was to culminate in the recognition in 1965, three years after the ending of the Algerian war, of the fact that the help which the French left-wing had given the Algerian independence movement had made no 'objective contribution' to its victory.[2]

In 1953, however, when he provided a long commentary linking together the articles which several other writers and journalists had contributed to a book about Henri Martin, he was clearly convinced that a vigorous presentation of facts and arguments could influence public opinion and thus affect political action. Henri Martin had joined the Resistance movement in France at the age of seventeen, in 1945, and subsequently transferred to the Navy. On discovering, when he was sent to Indochina, that he was expected to fight to keep people under French control and not to liberate them from the Japanese, he made three separate attempts to buy himself out. Each time, his request was refused, and in 1949, in the naval barracks at Toulon, he began to distribute tracts against the war. In 1950, he was sentenced to five year's imprisonment, and when the Communist party launched an appeal for his release, in 1951, he became a symbol for the general opposition to the war which the French were waging to retain control of what is now North and South Vietnam. Sartre's presentation of the case for his release is, essentially, a political one, and his principal target the French government's attempt to keep its empire by force of arms. It is not that he neglects the additional ammunition offered by the technical irregularities of Henri Martin's trial. Bourgeois society, as Lenin once remarked, has given itself rules which the revolutionary writer must try to use to make it strangle itself. But Sartre's practice as a committed writer has always been to concentrate on the politics, and in the condemnation of Henri Martin he saw a symbol of the whole disastrous colonial policy which was leading France not only to sacrifice her best men, but also to abandon all pretence of being a democratic country. In 1954, after the military defeat of Dien Bien Phu, the Indochinese war ended with the Geneva conference which divided the country into North and South Vietnam and effectively ended French colonialism in South East Asia. The problem of French North Africa remained, however, and the uprising in the Aurès mountains, in Algeria, on the night of 31 October–1 November marked the beginning of another colonial war in which Sartre and his team of writers on Les Temps Modernes played an even more active role than they had done in Indochina.

It was indeed Algeria which presented the greatest problem. Unlike Tunisia and Morocco, which became independent in 1954 and 1955, it was officially not a colony but France. The three départements of Alger, Constantine and Oran were, in theory at any rate, as much an integral part of France as the Pas-de-Calais or the Loire inférieure, and the whole French revolutionary tradition is based on the concept of a republic which is one and indivisible.

It was, however, on the contrast between theory and practice that
Sartre and the many left wing writers who shared his views
laid most emphasis in their opposition to the policy of keeping
Algeria French. Everyone, even the government supporters,
recognized that the million and a half Europeans had an immensely
higher standard of living than the nine million Arabs. But where
the apologists of *L'Algérie Française* explained this contrast as an
inevitable result of the coexistence of two civilizations at
different stages in their economic development, Sartre regarded
it as a product of a system which aimed quite consciously at the
exploitation of the original Arab inhabitants for the exclusive
benefit of the European landowners and the economy of metropolitan France. In an article entitled '*Le Colonialisme est un
Système*', he pointed out that during the nineteenth century the
French had used a variety of legal subterfuges to rob the
Algerians of all the best land. They had done so largely because
industry was too inefficient to compete in world markets, and
needed a group of tame consumers if it was to survive. This is very
close to the economic explanation of imperialism put forward by
Lenin, and Sartre also supports Lenin's view from an unexpected
source: he quotes the nineteenth-century statesman Jules Ferry
as justifying the colonization of Algeria by the need for the French
to create markets.[3] Sartre's later remark that 'the bourgeois of the
last century is quite consistently ignoble in all his activities'[4]
occurs in *La Critique de la Raison Dialectique* when he is actually
discussing European colonization, and reveals a much greater
readiness to argue on moral grounds than ever showed itself in his
analysis of Stalinism. However, the colonial system whereby the
French state 'gives the Arab lands to the *colons* in order to create a
purchasing power which will enable the industries of Metropolitan
France to sell them their products', and where 'the *colons* sell the
fruits of the stolen earth on the French Metropolitan market'
has ceased to pay dividends. Indeed, by obliging France to keep an
army of 400,000 men in Algeria, it is now 'turning against the
colonizing nation', and the French are, to use a phrase from *La
Critique de la Raison Dialectique*, caught in the 'hell of the
pratico-inerte'.

Nothing could be further from Charles Schweitzer's concept
of literature than this article, originally given as a speech at a
meeting in January 1956 and overflowing with facts and figures.
Neither was it Sartre's only contribution to the campaign against
the Algerian war. In June 1957, a Communist journalist, Henri
Alleg, had been arrested by French paratroops in Algeria and
kept prisoner for a month. During that time, he had been brutally
tortured, and had seen many other prisoners, both Arabs and
Europeans, subjected to the same treatment. In February 1958, he
published an account of his experiences in a book entitled

La Question which was immediately banned. Sartre's preface to it, *Une Victoire*, appeared in *L'Express* on 6 March 1958, and the whole issue of this left-wing weekly review was seized by the police. Like *L'Affaire Henri Martin, Une Victoire* is a political tract.[5] At the basis of the systematic use of torture in Algeria, Sartre recognizes a more fundamental project than the mere collection of information. The very aim of colonization, he argues, is to transform the natives into subhuman creatures. Their only function will then be to serve the 'men by divine right' of the colonizing nation, and torture is a weapon exactly suited to this ambition. Torture is at the very heart of the Algerian war, because what it seeks to destroy, in the individual victim, is the silence and resistance of a whole people. But, argues Sartre, when a man like Alleg succeeds in keeping his mouth under torture, he reduces the terrible 'archangels of anger' to their real status: that of cowards caught up in a system which they cannot control, victims of a war that they can win only by denying their own humanity.

Perhaps because it sees torture in a specifically political context, *Une Victoire* is a much better contribution than *Morts sans Sépulture* to the study of what Sartre calls 'a pox (*une vérole*) ravaging the whole of our epoch'. Although Sartre makes no mention of the coincidence between Alleg's experience and his own argument in *L'Etre et le Néant* that man remains free even under torture, there is no doubt that torture exercises such a fascination upon him precisely because it is an 'extreme situation' in which human freedom shows itself in its purest form. Sartre did not, however, limit himself, in his opposition to the Algerian war, to denouncing the use of torture. When the French population in Algiers, aided and abetted by the French army, set up a 'Committee of Public Safety' on 13 May 1958, thus beginning the process which was to bring General de Gaulle back to power, Sartre was one of the most forceful critics of what *Les Temps Modernes* called the 'pronunciamento general who, for all his talk about grandeur, reduces France to the level of a nineteenth-century South American dictatorship'.[6] In September 1958, he criticized the proposed new régime of the Fifth Republic as a 'Constitution of Contempt',[7] and spoke several times in public of what he saw as the imposition of a new form of government on France by the blackmailer's argument that its rejection would bring the paratroops now in Algeria floating down from the sky to attack Paris. In 1958 and 1959, the Algerian tail was wagging the French dog with more than usual vigour, and the particular example of the *pratico-inerte* constituted by French North Africa dominated French life as nothing had done since 1945.

What, at the moment of writing, is Sartre's last play, stemmed directly from his campaign against the Algerian war, and is perhaps the best example in his work of how he manages to combine political commitment with the general study of the human condition which characterizes existentialist literature. *Les Séquestrés d'Altona* is not, however, simply a play directed against the Algerian war and inspired in its plot and structure by the concepts developed in *La Critique de la Raison Dialectique*. It is a *summa* of all Sartre's major imaginative themes, from sequestration to fatherhood, from bad faith to Christianity, from the struggle to possess which takes the name of love, to the desire to justify one's acts; from incest to madness, from the conflict between imagination and reality to the denunciation of the bourgeoisie, and from the obsession with shellfish to the awareness of the future as an unpredictable source of moral judgment. It is, moreover, the only one of his works to be set in Germany, the country whose language he acquired as a child from the Schweitzer side of his family and whose mode of philosophical thinking he has done more than anyone else to acclimatize in France.

ii

Les Séquestrés d'Altona was produced at the Théâtre de la Renaissance on 23 September 1959. In spite of its length – even after drastic cuts, it still lasted almost four hours – it proved very successful with both press and public, and ran until 4 June 1960. Officially there was no literary censorship in the Fifth Republic. Nevertheless, a play openly directed against the policy of Algérie Française would certainly have been banned by some legal subterfuge such as the refusal of the police to guarantee the physical safety of the actors (an open invitation to right-wing demonstrators to disrupt performances), and Sartre chose, as he had done with *Les Mouches*, to express his ideas by allegory. The play is set in Germany in 1959, and describes the efforts made by a German officer to hide from himself the real significance of the tortures he inflicted on a number of Russian partisans during World War II. Since 1946, Frantz von Gerlach has lived shut away in a garret in the large house which his father owns at Altona, a suburb of Hamburg. He is looked after by his sister Leni, with whom he is committing incest, and his deliberately prolonged illusion that the prosperous Germany of 1959 is still a heap of rubble, is encouraged by her. The play ends when he is forced to abandon this particular form of bad faith, and has to recognize that Germany has become the most prosperous country in Western Europe precisely because of the defeat which he claims to have been desperately trying to avoid by the tortures he inflicted on the partisans. In the France of 1959, the analogy with the situation in Algeria was certainly obvious to a foreign spectator. By then, France was spending over two million pounds a day on a war she could not possibly win. Like Frantz von Gerlach, her soldiers were 'sacrificing their military honour to the need for victory',[8] and yet appeared highly likely to find themselves one day in exactly his position. They too would have to recognize that their crimes had served only to postpone a providential defeat, and one which gave their country a prosperity that victory could never have provided.

As it was, however, it appears that few people who saw the play in 1959 or 1960 recognized *Les Séquestrés d'Altona* as quite so transparent an allegory of the Algerian problem.[9] This may have been because the economic advantages of retaining Algeria had less place in the official justification for the war than the need to protect the French population against Arab imperialism, but it may also have been a result of the large number of other themes which Sartre put into his play. Frantz is not only sequestered as Sartre himself was in his childhood, and as Pierre is in *La Chambre* or Marcelle in the first volume of *Les Chemins de la Liberté*. Like the Garcin of *Huis Clos*, he is caught between two women, his sister Leni and his sister-in-law Johanna. The first is prepared to love him as he is but only on condition that she can possess him absolutely; while the second can love him only in the imaginary universe created by his lies and simulated madness, and turns against him as soon as reality breaks in. Frantz lives in his own world. There, he sees himself as a man specially chosen to bear witness on behalf of the twentieth century before the 'Tribunal of Crabs' which will, he proclaims, be the only form of life in the thirtieth century, and there is a very Sartrean reason why Johanna should be attracted by this semi-magical universe. Before her marriage, she had been a famous actress and film-star, but had always suffered from the impossibility of seeing her own beauty as other people saw it. What Frantz offers her, in his enclosed world, is the chance of grasping this beauty, almost holding it in the palm of her hand, through the very intensity with which he looks at her. So long as she can believe Frantz's 'official' reason for what happened near Smolensk in February 1944 – that he refused, through an excess of sensibility, to torture the partisans, and is therefore guilty for the continued ruin of Germany – she can escape from the real world where this possession of her own beauty always eludes her. But when Leni, determined that Frantz shall belong to nobody but herself, destroys Johanna's illusions by telling her the truth, while at the same time abolishing Frantz's imaginary world by showing him a newspaper describing the von Gerlach contribution to the West German 'economic miracle', their mutual bad faith can no longer exist. Johanna goes back to her mediocre husband Werner, while Frantz, confronted by a world in which none of his actions makes any sense, goes off with his father to commit suicide in a car-ride to which Sartre gives the associations of a *Götterdämmerung*.

Like *Les Mains Sales, Les Séquestrés d'Altona* thus ends with a
hero unable to assume responsibility for what he has done. Had
Germany really been permanently reduced to the desolation
which Frantz had seen in 1946, his acts would have fitted into the
same kind of pattern which Goetz foresees by his readiness to
stab the mutinous soldier at the end of *Le Diable et le Bon Dieu*:
one where violence is justified by the need to create or avoid a
real situation. As it is, however, Frantz's action in torturing the
partisans is more like Hugo's shooting of Hoederer. Because of a
twist in the direction history has taken, it becomes a crime which
nobody wants, least of all the person responsible for it. The break
with the pattern apparently established by *Le Diable et le Bon Dieu,
Kean* and *Nekrassov* is obvious, and there is a phrase in *Une
Victoire* which suggests why Sartre should have virtually repeated
the ending of *Les Mains Sales* in what is, in other respects, a very
left-wing play. In the 1958 preface to Alleg's book, he described
the Krushchev report to the Twentieth Party Congress as
'unimpeachable evidence' that torture had been an instrument of
public policy in Stalin's Russia.[10] Consequently, the situation of
Frantz von Gerlach represented, in 1959, more than the immediate problem of the German officers who had served Hitler's
Ostpolitik or the future dilemma of the French soldiers devoting
themselves to L'Algérie Française. It ran parallel to that of
the sincere Communist who had believed the crimes of the
Stalin period to be essential to the building up of socialism, but
who discovered, on hearing the Krushchev report, that they
stemmed from a personality cult which had harmed rather than
advanced the real interests of the Russian people. Just as the
apologist for Stalinism would switch from denouncing reports of
Communist atrocities as fabrications of the bourgeois press to
arguing that no one could make an omelette without breaking
eggs, so Frantz alternates between denying that he has ever
tortured anyone and claiming that only by torture could a
disastrous defeat be avoided; so that even the form of his bad faith
reflects the Communist dilemma. Once committed, his acts also
constituted a framework from which there was no escape, exactly
as Stalinism saddled the Russian leaders with a ghost that walked
triumphantly in Budapest on 4 November 1956. For all Sartre's
acceptance of Marxist philosophy it would seem that he felt a good
deal less confident about the chances of viable political action in
1958 and 1959 than he had done between 1952 and 1956.

It was, however, less the possible analogy with Stalinism than
the presence of Sartre's more personal and obsessional themes
which distracted both the critics' and the public's attention from the
relevance of *Les Séquestrés d'Altona* to the Algerian war. Almost
everyone noticed the similarity with *Huis Clos* and *La Chambre*,
while Frantz's vision of a future inhabited solely by shellfish was

also seen as a move back to the horrified animal imagery of *La Nausée*. Just as in *La Nausée*, however, the imagery was highly relevant to the ideas Sartre was expressing. He regards it as peculiar to the twentieth century that we should be intensely aware that future generations will certainly judge and probably condemn us.[11] Indeed, within the play itself, Johanna belongs to a generation which is already beyond the point where it can understand the pressures to which men of Frantz's age were subjected, and the horror with which she recoils from him shows how right he is to anticipate the verdict of 'guilty'. By no stretch of the imagination can we tell what shellfish might be thinking, if indeed they think at all, and the future is equally inscrutable. Frantz himself is in bad faith throughout the play, and like Jean Genet's quest for sainthood, his obsession with how the future will think of us is a means of escaping from the present judgment of his fellows. Yet his bad faith, again like Genet's, leads to an expression of what it is like to be alive in mid-twentieth-century Europe, caught in a situation where we are most profoundly alienated by what we ourselves have done, where we are at one and the same time both victim, judge and executioner in a history that has lost all meaning, and where the infinite mercy of God is replaced by the implacable hostility of our sons.

Sartre wrote *Les Séquestrés d'Altona* while he was actually working on *Les Mots*, and the preoccupation with his own childhood experience is most evident in the importance which he gives to Frantz's father. Old von Gerlach has indeed dominated his son and 'ridden piggy-back upon him through his life', just as Sartre imagines all fathers so doing in *Les Mots*; the possibly fruitful father–son relationship which seems capable of arising between Hoederer and Hugo in *Les Mains Sales* turns in *Les Séquestrés d'Altona* into a study of how a father's lust for power can ruin his own life as well as that of his son. Between 1933 and 1945, von Gerlach served the Nazis, and since 1946 has grown even more prosperous by serving the Americans. But he is now dying of cancer of the throat, and this illness is a physical symbol of how capitalism is, quite literally, strangled by its own success. Although he is head of one of the largest ship-building yards in Europe, he has lost all real power. The empire which he had created for his son, and for whose sake he had brought Frantz into the world, has escaped from his control. As he rather bitterly remarks, he has to pay professional managers to tell him what orders he should give. Like the French colonists who established so effective a rule in Algeria that France seemed in 1959 unable to disengage herself from the cancerous growth in her own body, von Gerlach is the victim of the system he has spent his life creating, and this strikes back at him through the son whom he loves most dearly. The war which his support for Hitler made inevitable led to the moment when Frantz had to choose between torturing the Russian partisans and depriving the men under his command of their opportunity to escape. But this choice was not one which Frantz could take with the same calm awareness of what he was doing that characterized Bariona, Oreste or Goetz. Once, in 1941, his father had put him into a position where, after a childhood devoted to making him a 'prince of this world', he experienced total impotence. When the crisis arose on the Russian front, he was dominated both by this memory and by the 'bitter taste for power' which his father had instilled into him. Frantz tortures the partisans less as an act of deliberate policy than because of the psychological pressures building up inside him, and in this respect the play seems to represent a change in Sartre's work from an insistence on freedom to the acknowledgment that our behaviour can in certain circumstances be predetermined.

This is again a point of resemblance between *Les Séquestrés d'Altona* and *Les Mots*. Just as Sartre's future was decided for him by the sudden transformation of Charles Schweitzer from an amiable buffoon into a stern father surrogate, so Frantz's actions are presented for much of the play as stemming directly from the influence which his authoritarian father had on him. However, Sartre also makes Frantz recognize, in the crucial last act, that when he tortured the partisans it was during 'a moment of independence',[12] and *Les Séquestrés d'Altona* has more than a touch of his old insistence on the unbreakable link between liberty and responsibilty. Indeed, Frantz would not have locked himself away in order to escape from his guilt unless he knew, in his heart of hearts, that he could have done otherwise at that crucial moment near Smolensk when there was nobody else to give him orders. There is never any real doubt in the spectator's mind that Frantz more than suspects the truth about the prosperous Germany which lies outside his shuttered windows, and as in *L'Etre et le Néant*, it is the existence of bad faith which underlines the fact of human freedom. In the very last scene, when Frantz sees his father again after the thirteen years during which he had allowed only Leni to come near him, his behaviour is still inspired by a desire to escape from the awareness of his responsibility. He agrees to go off and commit suicide only on one condition: that von Gerlach should acknowledge that he, the father, is responsible for everything. Frantz knows that he can believe this only for a very short time, and consequently insists that they kill themselves straight away. Yet although this is again a conscious decision on his part, his situation, like Hugo's, is so desperate that there is no other solution open to him. Moreover, the resemblance between Frantz's situation and some of the arguments put forward in *La Critique de la Raison Dialectique*, strengthens the impression that Sartre's view of liberty undergoes a fundamental change at this period in his career.

Thus Sartre gives the example, at one point, of a woman working in a factory making the DOP cosmetic products acquiring a chronic eczema because of the chemicals she handles, and consoling herself by taking a lover. When she gets pregnant, and has no money to bring up her child alone, she takes what could, theoretically, be presented as the free decision to have an abortion. Nevertheless, she is in a situation where there is no viable alternative, and to talk of freedom in such a context is a hollow mockery. Society has killed her child just as surely as if it had passed a law compelling her to have an abortion.[13] Frantz von Gerlach enjoyed a similarly restricted margin of choice, and Sartre's remark, in 1969, that he now looks back with bewildering incomprehension on his earlier statement that 'Whatever the circumstances, and wherever the site, a man is always free to choose to be a traitor or not'[14] concludes a development which begins with *Saint Genet, Comédien et Martyr* but becomes really important only with *Les Séquestrés d'Altona*. Neither is the highly ambiguous presentation of the debate between freedom and determinism the only feature of *Les Séquestrés d'Altona* which sets it apart from *Bariona*, *Les Mouches* or *Le Diable et le Bon Dieu*. Von Gerlach declares at one point that the Germans are 'victims of Luther', the prophet who has rendered them 'mad with pride',[15] and Frantz's social conditioning by his father is paralleled by what Sartre would call an 'interiorization' of a religious view of life which makes him the most Christian as well as the least genuinely free of all his heroes.

It could, of course, be argued that the predominance of Christian themes in *Les Séquestrés d'Altona* is part of an attempt at social realism which is fully consistent with the left-wing aspects of the play, its implied attack on l'Algérie française and its equation of successful capitalism with cancer. It is quite conceivable that a North German Protestant family should swear on the Bible and interlard its conversation with Old and New Testament references, and Sartre himself said that it was Frantz's 'Protestant conscience' which prevented him from accepting what he had done during the war. Yet the play is also overflowing with a Christian symbolism which certainly gives the Father and Frantz the mythical status of God and Man, and even, occasionally, that of God and Christ. Thus Frantz declares that his father 'created him in his own image', is referred to as the Prodigal son, tries to go one better than the disciples in remaining constantly awake, and is most concerned, throughout his thirteen year sequestration, at the way his father is judging him for his crimes. This religious symbolism is underlined by the suggestion that Frantz has become, by this stage in the play, almost as much

Christ as man. He conducts a parody of the Last Supper when Leni brings him a cake to celebrate his thirty-fourth birthday – it is perhaps no more than a coincidence that the traditional age of Christ at his crucifixion is thirty-three – and at another point he pretends to be amazed that his sweat has not turned to blood. His Christ-like status is also heightened by the fact that he sees himself, in the speeches which he delivers to the Crabs, as taking upon himself the sins of the whole world, and the ending of the play offers a curious inversion of the traditional relationship between God and Christ. Instead of the son being sacrificed to appease the wrath of an avenging deity, it is the father who acknowledges his guilt and accepts death in order to wipe out the sins of the son.[16]

Neither is this return to religious preoccupations the only metaphysical theme in *Les Séquestrés d'Altona*. Frantz has the 'speeches for the defence' which he spends his days and nights composing in his garret taken down on a tape-recorder, and the one he considers his best effort is played back as the curtain falls on the empty stage at the end of the play. A French critic noted in 1959 that the word for tape-recorder (*magnétophone*) inevitably recalled the device most frequently used for torturing prisoners in Algeria, the magneto of a field service telephone, and this apparently accidental pun heightens the relevance of the play to the Algerian problem.[17] The content of Frantz's last speech, however, presents the problem of violence in a much less political context. 'Our century would have been good,' he declaims 'if man had not been stalked by his cruel, immemorial enemy, by the flesh-eating species which had sworn his ruin, by the cunning, hairless beast, by man,' and his rhetoric is practically a word-for-word quotation from Sartre's discussion of violence in *La Critique de la Raison Dialectique*. 'Nothing', he writes there, 'neither microbes nor the Lords of the Jungle, can be more terrible for man than an intelligent, cruel, flesh-eating species, capable of understanding and outwitting human intelligence, and whose prime aim lies in the destruction of man. This species is obviously our own, comprehending itself in each individual through the intermediary of others in an environment dominated by scarcity.'[18] The violence in his own nature to which Frantz gave way when he tortured the partisans is not, in this context, a sign of any special wickedness either in him or in the political systems which he served or symbolized. It is the way he has to behave in a world whose basic rule remains 'Kill or starve', and Sartre's definition of violence in *La Critique de la Raison Dialectique* as 'interiorized scarcity' emphasizes the extent to which he regards conflict as an inevitable part of the human condition. Great though his horror of torture certainly is, whether he sees it in a philosophical or a political context, the theory of aggression which he puts forward in *La Critique de la Raison Dialectique* and translates into *Les Séquestrés d'Altona* suggests that there is no moral distinction between the Goetz who stabs the mutinous soldier at the end of *Le Diable et le Bon Dieu* and the Frantz who tortures the partisans. 'The beast was hiding', continues Frantz, 'we surprised its glance, suddenly, in our neighbour's inner eye; then, we struck him down. Legitimate self-defence. I surprised the beast, I struck, a man fell, in his dying eyes I saw the beast, still alive, I myself. One and one make one.' All acts of violence are the same, and whether man kills for the revolution or tortures to save his country, it is the same 'naked, hairless ape' who kills himself in the other person before trying to bear witness for his crime and abolish it with his own death. Neither Frantz nor his father are the straightforward fascist villains that Sartre's political opinions on French imperialism or Western capitalism would theoretically require them to be. They are tragic heroes, caught in a situation which they cannot understand, victims of their own acts and crucified by their own intentions, capable of understanding what is happening to them but not of transcending it, responsible for what they are and yet incapable of having done otherwise, prisoners at the bar of history and yet with no executioner but themselves, the last representatives of a Christian sensibility in a world where God is dead but neither history nor love can take His place.

iii

The problem of violence, treated in different ways throughout Sartre's work, was a dominant theme in French life in the years immediately following the production of *Les Séquestrés d'Altona*. The realization, early in 1960, that de Gaulle might well be planning to abandon Algeria led to the formation of the Organisation de l'Armée Secrète (OAS), an extremist organization determined to keep Algeria French at all costs. It aimed to achieve this aim partly by intensifying the war in Algeria itself through provocative attacks on Arab civilians, and partly by terrorizing anyone who, in metropolitan France, argued in favour of bringing the war to an end by a negotiated settlement. Two plastic bomb attacks were made by the OAS on Sartre's apartment in the rue Bonaparte, the first on 19 July 1961 and the second on 7 January 1962, and they can both be seen as connected with a demonstration in October 1961 when a number of ex-servicemen paraded up and down the Champs-Elysées proclaiming that he ought to be shot. The period between 1960 and 1962 was indeed one of the most highly political in the whole of Sartre's life. In 1957 his friend and disciple Francis Jeanson had organized a network of sympathizers prepared to offer aid and comfort to young Frenchmen who refused to do their military service in Algeria as well as to members of the Algerian Armée de Libération Nationale. Sartre had agreed with Jeanson's action at the time, and it was certainly consistent with the editorial 'Refus d'Obéissance, which *Les Temps Modernes* had published in October 1955. In August 1960 Sartre was also one of the principal signatories – though not the author – of the '*Manifeste du 121*', a tract in which 121 writers, journalists, actors, teachers and intellectuals declared that they 'respected and considered fully justified the refusal to bear arms against the Algerian people', whose 'cause was that of all free men'. The August number of *Les Temps Modernes* was seized by the police for giving the actual text of this manifesto, as well as the names of its signatories, but in September of the same year Sartre took another and less easily censored step to make his attitude on the Algerian war known to as wide a public as he could reach. Francis Jeanson's network had been discovered by the police, and he was coming up for trial.

It was on 20 September 1960 that Sartre declared, in a letter read to the Court, that had Jeanson asked him to do so he would have carried suitcases on behalf of the Algerian Front de Libération Nationale. In view of the fact that such suitcases could well have contained explosives, it was as complete an act of moral support as could be imagined for the acts of violence committed by the FLN.[19] In 1967, looking back on the Algerian war in the context of what he regarded as the comparable struggle being waged by the Vietcong, Sartre declared that he had always, between 1954 and 1962 'refused to accept the parallel between terrorist bomb attacks which were the only weapon at the disposal of the Algerians, and the exactions and actions of a rich army of 500,000 men occupying their country'[20] and his adoption of two standards, one to condemn imperialism and the other to condone revolt, has never been more explicit. In February 1962, when the violence in France stemmed from the efforts of the OAS to prevent a peaceful settlement of the Algerian problem, Sartre declared that one of his main objectives was to destroy the idea that the Left ought not to reply to violence by violence. Indeed, one sometimes has the impression that he would not have been heart-broken if the Algerian war had received a more violent solution than the one which General de Gaulle succeeded in imposing in June 1962.

The complete story of how France eventually freed herself of Algeria will not be known for some time, even after the publication of de Gaulle's memoirs for the years between 1958 and 1962. What he actually did, however, is not in dispute. By using his immense prestige both with the army and with the vast majority of the French nation, he manoeuvred the supporters of l'Algérie française into the position where it was they and not the left wing who appeared as the opponents of French unity. In fact, the Evian agreements of June 1962, which put an end to the Algerian war, gave the Algerian nationalists the complete independence which Sartre and his allies had always declared that they ought to have, and it is a little disappointing to find nowhere, either in Sartre's own works, or in *Les Temps Modernes* any acknowledgment of what de Gaulle did achieve. It is true that de Gaulle carried out the policy of the French left wing by a series of referenda which, as *Les Temps Modernes* argued at the time, effectively prevented the French people from playing any role at all in the government they had elected and which was supposedly responsible to them. De Gaulle also pointedly declined the support of the left, and the frequency with which *Les Temps Modernes* was seized by the police between 1960 and 1962[21] certainly justifies the lack of enthusiasm which Sartre and his friends showed for his day-to-day policies. But the long-term results of de Gaulle's tactics were, as far as Algeria was concerned, exactly what Sartre wanted, and Sartre's refusal to acknowledge this seems particularly churlish in view of the striking similarities between de Gaulle's performance as a politician and the principles enunciated by his own favourite hero, Hoederer. If he did not actually lie to the troops, de Gaulle kept remarkably quiet about his real intentions, and he certainly shared Hoederer's view that to allow ordinary people the genuine possibility of deciding what was to happen next was a luxury that could be postponed until the immediate struggle was over. Perhaps what is most admirable about de Gaulle's Algerian policy, however, is that it did show how one particular instance of the *pratico-inerte* could be overcome. When he came to power in 1958, de Gaulle looked to almost all observers like a man who would be equally controlled by his own past record as a nationalist leader and by the army and European settlers who had overthrown the Fourth Republic. Instead, he overcame both obstacles and showed that some western politicians could exorcise their ghosts, however much the eastern dictators might still be haunted by theirs.

As far as Sartre's relationship with his own country was concerned, the last few years of the Algerian war were among the unhappiest in his life. He was profoundly disappointed by the overwhelming majority which de Gaulle received in the referendum which accepted the proposed constitution of the Fifth Republic in September 1958, and his health was affected to the point where *Les Séquestrés d'Altona*, originally planned for autumn 1958, had to be postponed to the following year. Simone de Beauvoir describes him as taking so much of a drug called corydrane in order to give himself enough energy to write *La Critique de la Raison Dialectique* that he fell seriously ill,[22] and he perhaps put this particular aspect of his experience into

Les Séquestrés d'Altona, where Frantz von Gerlach keeps himself awake by taking benzedrine and washing it down with champagne.

Each summer, Sartre and Simone de Beauvoir continued to find refuge from the unpleasant atmosphere of France in the more welcoming climate of Italy, and in 1963 Sartre went so far as to say that he would join the Italian Communist Party if he were living there permanently.[23] In France, both Sartre and Simone de Beauvoir felt that they were living once again in an occupied country, and that for the second time since 1945. In the late forties and early fifties, they had already looked upon the American troops sent to join NATO as renewing the occupation of 1940–1945,[24] and during the closing years of the Algerian war it was even worse. Indeed, the French paratroops seemed so much like Nazi soldiers that Sartre had no compunction in translating what he called in 1958 the 'decomposition which can arise inside a family as a result of the silence of a national service man on his return from Algeria' into what was ostensibly the purely German context of *Les Séquestrés d'Altona*. Moreover, Sartre and Simone de Beauvoir could no longer count on the same universal opposition to the 'occupying forces' which had existed in France between 1940 and 1944. They were well-known figures in French society, and when they ate in a restaurant, their fellow diners would turn round and manifest their displeasure at the views which *Les Temps Modernes* had been expressing on the Algerian problem. The government was also skilful enough to abstain from making them into martyrs, and did not arrest them for treason. Sartre deliberately courted arrest by his attitude at the Jeanson trial, but nevertheless had to endure the humiliation of seeing many of the teachers and civil servants who had signed the *Manifeste du 121* lose their jobs while he himself went scot-free. In his preface to a revised edition of Paul Nizan's *Aden-Arabie* in 1960, he spoke of the 'total impotence' which now afflicted men of the left in 'this backward province known as France',[25] and the disillusion which he felt for the France of the Algerian war did more than encourage him in his liking for Italy. It led to his visit to Cuba in the early spring of 1960, as well as to his admiration for the writers and politicians of the other countries of the Third World which were beginning to escape from European domination.

Sartre spent just over a month in Cuba, and expressed his enthusiasm for Castro's revolution in a number of different publications. A series of articles appeared in *France-Soir* – perhaps rather a strange choice for the author of *Nekrassov* – between 28 June and 15 July 1960; he gave several press conferences in both America and France; and he also wrote a book about Cuba which has appeared in English and Spanish but not, curiously enough, in French. Sartre apparently got on very well with Castro, and regarded his revolution as a model for other countries. It certainly fitted remarkably well into the theories of *La Critique de la Raison Dialectique*, especially into Sartre's view of what happens when people escape from the relationship which he describes as 'seriality' – waiting at a bus-stop is his own illustration of what he means – and group themselves into dynamic units capable of political action. He regards such movements as occurring most readily in a revolutionary situation, when the oppressed feel themselves threatened by the forces of the established order. It is then that they fuse into a living group which asserts its identity by an oath that its members make to support one another, and *La Critique de la Raison Dialectique* analyses this phenomenon in detail with examples taken from the first French revolution. When the Cubans recognized their communal identity in Castro, they too escaped from the 'serialized impotence' imposed on them by the various régimes which had collaborated with American imperialism, and became capable of political action.

If Sartre was enthusiastic about Cuba partly because of the confirmation which it gave to his ideas of how an ideal revolution established its power, what he saw as the failure of decolonization in the Belgian Congo in 1960 and 1961 reinforced his view that no revolution could triumph without an apprenticeship of violence which welded the members of the newly formed group together and thus enabled them to emerge from their 'seriality'. In 1963, Sartre published a long article about the African revolutionary leader Patrice Lumumba, Prime Minister of the ex-Belgian Congo until he fell from power and was assassinated in January 1961. Sartre has no doubt as to who was guilty for his death. The Belgians, French and English, aided by the big mining companies and abetted by the 'abject partiality' of Dag Hammarskjöld, actually arranged for Lumumba to be murdered, but there were other culprits as well: the 'black bourgeoisie' which sold out to neo-colonialism, and the Belgians who gave independence to the Congo before a violent revolutionary struggle had had time to forge the unity of the new nation by its opposition to colonial rule.[26] It might, Sartre argues, have been a reasonable solution gradually to replace the colonial authorities by educated Congolese, but this would have been a 'reformist solution, coldly conceived by a statesman weighing the arguments for and against'. It would, therefore, have been wrong, and what was really needed, as Sartre made clear in 1961 in his preface to Franz Fanon's *Les Damnés de la Terre*, is something very different: a movement in which, as in Nkrumah's Ghana, 'the struggle is organized in secret and in the heat of battle (*à chaud*)'. What then emerges is a true culture: 'A revolution; that is to say, something forged in the fire.'[27]

The cult of violence which characterizes Sartre's thinking on colonialism reaches its height in this preface to Fanon's book, and is best summed up in a phrase taken from it: 'To shoot a European is to kill two birds with one stone, abolishing at one and the same time an oppressor and a victim of oppression. What is left behind is a dead man and a free man; the survivor, for the first time in his life, feels a truly national soil beneath his feet.'[28] Such an argument is perhaps the logical extension of the vision in the *Réflexions sur la Question Juive* of the authentic Jew affirming his true identity for the first time by standing up to the anti-semite. Nevertheless, like Sartre's admiration for Che Guevara and apparent support for the US 'Weathermen', it also bears witness to an almost pathological exasperation both with Western society and with anything but the most extreme revolutionary tradition in Europe.[29]

On a more personal level, Sartre's determination to ally himself most closely with those whom his own country had exploited most shamelessly, led him in 1965 to take what might seem at first sight a rather curious step. On 18 March he legally adopted a young Algerian girl, Arlette El-Kaïm. He had first met her in 1955, when her philosophy teacher at Versailles expressed disapproval of an essay in which Miss El-Kaïm, at that time a student preparing for the competitive examination to enter the Ecole normale supérieure de Sèvres, had spoken enthusiastically of Sartre's ideas. She had written to Sartre to ask him what he thought, and the relationship had developed from that basis. In 1967 his adopted daughter was to play an important secretarial role in Sartre's campaign against the Vietnam war. It was she who edited the summary of the conclusions reached by the Russell Tribunal, and prepared the English text entitled *On Genocide* by Jean-Paul Sartre. And a summary of the evidence and judgments of the International War Crimes Tribunal by Arlette El Kaim-Sartre.[30]

9 Literature, students and a conclusion

A theme which recurs in *Les Séquestrés d'Altona*, and gives the English translation of the play its title, is that of *Loser Wins*. It is a paradox which makes its first major appearance in Sartre's work in *Saint Genet, Comédien et Martyr*, where Sartre argues that Genet's cult of evil leads him to wish to fail, but that his very success in so doing leads to a triumph, and in *Les Séquestrés d'Altona* it has an obvious relevance to the idea that the most prosperous countries in the modern world are those which lose wars or colonies. At the end of *Les Mots*, after describing the disillusion which he now feels about his literary career, Sartre nevertheless raises the possibility that he too may triumph as a result of what he now considers to have been the wrong choice. 'Magnificent and stinking,' he writes, comparing himself in yet another classical reference to the Philoctetes whose bow was the only weapon capable of guaranteeing victory to the Greeks, but whose wounds smelt so vile that he had to be left alone on an island, 'this sick man gave away even his bow without any condition; but you can be sure that, underneath, he expected his reward'.[1] Although, as he said in 1964, one of his aims in writing *Les Mots* was to show young people who dreamed of becoming writers how such an ambition had taken, in his case, the form of a neurosis, the very success of his autobiography bears out how true the paradox of 'loser wins' can be. The two hundred or so pages in which he denounces his literary calling contain some of the best prose he has ever written, and *Les Mots* was more favourably received by the French critics than any other of Sartre's works. 'The congratulations,' wrote one reviewer, 'go to Madame Sartre *mère*, it is she to whom the book is most suitably dedicated,'[2] and Anne-Marie is indeed the only person to emerge from *Les Mots* with any degree of credit. The actual dedication reads '*À Madame Z*', but Anne-Marie Sartre was still alive – she died in 1969, at an age which did credit to the traditional longevity of the Schweitzers – and it is a matter of infinite regret to all present-day readers of her son's work that it is impossible to find out what she thought of it all. Perhaps posterity will be more fortunate.

Les Mots was the only one of Sartre's books to be translated into Russian within a year of its original publication, and it also had the unusual privilege of being enthusiastically reviewed in the *Liternaturnaia Gazetta*. In his preface to the publication of the translation in *Novy Mir*, in October and November 1964, Sartre wrote that he wanted people to read his book for what it was, 'the attempt to destroy a myth',[3] and in this respect he openly acknowledged how right Bernard Frank had been to review the book in *France-Observateur* as a deliberate attack on the Romantic idea of what Baudelaire calls '*le vert paradis des amours enfantines*'.[4] Childhood, for Sartre, was the most miserable of experiences, and the whole book is shot through with nostalgia that he was not like the athletic, well-integrated games-players of the Luxembourg gardens. Nevertheless, the cossetted upbringing which he received is not all that untypical of some French children even today. It was even more common in the early years of the present century, and André Gide's famous '*Familles, je vous hais*', which struck so responsive a chord in the adolescents of the twenties and thirties, is a reaction against the same tendency to treat children as miniature grown-ups which so appals Sartre when he looks back at his own childhood. Perhaps this is why *Les Mots* arouses such different reactions in French and English readers. While those brought up in the Anglo-Saxon tradition, where children are expected to play, recoil in horrified amazement from this account of a child stretched on the Procrustes' bed of adult misconceptions, French readers feel a less vehement disapproval. What they recognize is an extreme version of the upbringing imposed upon themselves, and this recognition is all the greater if, like Sartre, they belong to a particular section of the professional or intellectual middle class. Certainly, few of the French critics who reviewed *Les Mots* thought it worthwhile to comment either on its implicit appeal for an education where children learn more from mixing with their equals than from imitating adults, or on the other corollary to Sartre's account of his first ten years: that the way to avoid making people into revolutionaries is to give them a genuinely democratic education. Yet this may have been less because the French themselves are not interested in children than because Sartre himself moves fairly quickly away from the day-to-day details of his childhood to present more general considerations about literature. He said later that he wanted to avoid the picturesque and anecdotal aspect of autobiography, and concentrate instead on how the period in which he was brought up showed itself in the choice he made to be a particular kind of writer. His refusal of the Nobel Prize for Literature in October 1964 concentrated attention even further upon the relevance of *Les Mots* to the problem of why people write books, and added to a debate about the nature and limits of literature which, in 1963 and 1964, preoccupied the French literary world almost as much as the publication of *Qu'est-ce que la Littérature?* had done in 1947 and 1948. Virtually every literary review carried long articles discussing Sartre's action, and on 9 December 1964, 8000 young people went to hear him speak at a debate organized by the Communist review *Clarté* on the theme '*Que peut la littérature?*'[5]

Sartre is the first author ever to have refused the Nobel Prize for Literature, and was apparently surprised to discover that the Swedish Academy always awarded it without asking whether the person wanted a prize or not.[6] The situation at the moment is that Sartre, as his own words in *Who's Who in France* point out, has refused the prize 'for personal and objective reasons', while the Nobel Academy considers that the award has been made to him. A parallel if less well-known relationship exists between Sartre and the University of Leeds. In 1967, he sent a telegram accepting an honorary doctorate, but did not come to the graduation ceremony.[7] He refused the Nobel Prize partly because, as he said in his official statement to the press in October 1964, he had always made a point of not accepting official honours. But he also refused because he considered that the writer ought to use only his own ability to handle language in order to propagate his ideas, and not the authority of any established institution. He would, he added, have refused the Lenin prize for the same reasons. Moreover, because it was always given either to Western writers or to Russian heretics like Pasternak, the Nobel Prize had acquired certain political connotations. If it had been offered to him just after he had signed the *Manifeste du 121*, he would have accepted, for this would have served a cause which deserved and needed help. In 1964, however, his acceptance would imply that he had been 'recuperated' by Western society.[8]

Convincing though such arguments may be on a general plane, Sartre's refusal of the Nobel Prize can also be linked to the disillusionment about literature which he had begun to feel some ten years earlier. He explained, in one of the interviews which he gave shortly after the publication of *Les Mots*, that when he had begun to write his autobiography in the early 1950s he had been on the point of regretting his decision ever to be a writer, and Simone de Beauvoir reports that he told her, around 1954, that '*la littérature, c'est de la merde.*'[9] Yet although he claims to have realized by 1963 that there was 'no reason to drag some unfortunate individual through the mire just because he writes',[10] *Les Mots* certainly reflects the disappointment which he must have felt at realizing how little immediate influence literature had. The Indochinese war had ended because the French army was defeated in the field at Dien-Bien-Phu, and Sartre himself recognized that Algeria achieved its independence because the FLN fought off the French army long enough to persuade de Gaulle that the game was not worth the candle. In April 1964 he told Jacqueline Piatier, of *Le Monde*, that 'by the side of a child dying of hunger, *La Nausée* weighs nothing at all', and it is perhaps significant that he has not published any major work since that date.

What appears, at the moment, to be Sartre's last play was an adaptation of Euripides' *The Trojan Women*. This enjoyed immense success when produced by Michel Cacoyannis at the Théâtre National Populaire in March 1965, and was certainly a brilliant recasting in contemporary language of a classical text. Euripides had written the tragedy of Hecuba and her women as a protest against the imperialism shown by the Athens in mounting the Sicilian expedition. If there was any doubt left in the minds of the many who had seen *Les Troyennes* as to what contemporary situation it actually referred to, this was rapidly dispelled by Sartre's stand against American policy in Vietnam. He had already remarked in 1965 that the play was 'a condemnation of war in general and of colonial expeditions in particular',[11] and when, in April of the same year, he suddenly cancelled his proposed visit to America, he crossed the i's and dotted the t's with a degree of vigour unusual even for him. He had been invited to give a series of lectures on Flaubert and Kant at Cornell University, but in an interview entitled '*Il n'y a plus de dialogue possible*', he declared that the American bombing of North Vietnam now made it impossible for any 'European intellectual who identified himself with the Third World' to ask for a visa. America was now 'a country entirely conditioned by the myths of imperialism and anti-Communism', and there was no hope of any American liberal influencing his country's policy. Indeed, he continued, 'I consider such a man, who has my respect, as *un damné de la terre*. He totally disapproves of what is being done in his name, and his action is completely ineffective, at least on a short-term basis.'[12] David Grossvogel, one of the University teachers who had originally issued the invitation, wrote an open letter to Sartre contrasting his rigid and uncompromising attitude with Hoederer's readiness to get his hands dirty, but Sartre stuck to his decision. In a message published in the Italian Communist newspaper *L'Unità*, Sartre insisted that the American government would have to consider the Vietcong as the only valid representatives of the South Vietnamese people, just as the French had finally been obliged to recognize the Gouvernement Provisoire de la République Algérienne, and in November 1966 he declared his support for the International Tribunal Against War Crimes in Vietnam recently established by Lord Russell. The Western democracies themselves, he argued, had created the notion of war crime by the Nuremburg tribunal which had passed sentence on the Nazis in 1946. The aim of Lord Russell and his supporters was simply to oblige America to apply her own standards to her own behaviour.

Such standards were not, he inferred, equally applicable to the Vietcong, for he refused to 'put on the same level the action of a group of poverty-stricken peasants, hunted down and obliged to

impose an iron discipline within their own ranks, and that of an
immense army supported by an over-industrialized country of
200 million inhabitants'.[13] In his open letter to de Gaulle, on
3 May 1967, after the Russell Tribunal had been refused
permission to meet officially in France, Sartre protested against
the fact that de Gaulle's letter to him had begun with the words
'*Cher maître*'.[14] This, he argued, showed that de Gaulle recognized
him as a writer and not as President of the Tribunal. It could,
nevertheless, be maintained that Sartre's readiness to take part in
the proceeding of this tribunal was significant only because he
was a writer, and that de Gaulle's mode of address was
consequently fully justified. In his campaign against Stalinism,
as in his attacks against French colonial policy, Sartre had always
kept his eye very firmly on the political ball. What he then used
was not his prestige as a writer but his ability either to marshal
facts and present arguments in books and articles, or to arouse
emotion by imaginative works. Perhaps because his moral indignation strangled him, he did nothing comparable in the case of
Vietnam.

Whatever the rights and wrongs of his violent opposition
to American policy, Sartre's implicit rejection of *la littérature
engagée* in 1963 – 'For a long time', he wrote in *Les Mots*, 'I took
my pen for a sword. Now I acknowledge how impotent we are'[15]
– does make his later political activity less interesting than his earlier
campaigns. Most of what he thinks is rather predictable, in the
sense that it is no surprise to learn that he is against apartheid, a
supporter of the people he calls the 'Venezuelan resistance
fighters', in favour of the legalization of the Greek Communist
Party, an opponent of Franco, in sympathy with liberation
movements in Bolivia and Guadeloupe, and acutely conscious of
the dangers of a fascist revival in Europe.[16] Yet there was one
occasion on which he did not adopt the same attitude as most
other writers and intellectuals of the extreme left. In June 1967
Les Temps Modernes published a remarkably well-balanced
special number on the Arab-Israeli conflict, to which Sartre
himself contributed a preface entitled '*Nos exigences contradictoires.*' It was, he wrote, impossible for men of the left to condemn
either side. The Israelis belonged to the race which Hitler had
persecuted, and it was impossible to make any clear distinction
between enmity towards Israel and anti-semitism; but the links
between the European left and the Arab nations had been forged
during the struggle for Algerian independence and could not be
abandoned. Nevertheless, on 1 June 1967, Sartre did speak out
against those who 'identified Israel with an aggressive and
imperialist camp' while considering that the Arab states were
uniformly 'peace-loving and socialist'. Israel, he proclaimed, had
the right to exist, and must therefore not be denied access to

international waterways.[17] This obvious criticism of Egypt's attempt to blockade the Gulf of Akaba brought violent protests from the Arab states, and there are a number of possible reasons why Sartre chose to go against the prevailing current of left-wing thought. As he said in *'Nos exigences contradictoires'*, nobody could carry fair-mindedness to the point of supporting a war of extermination, and he may simply have recognized Arab policy for what it was. Alternatively, he may have wished to dissociate himself from de Gaulle's description of the Jews as *'un peuple d'élite, sûr de lui-même et dominateur'* and of the support for the Arab cause implied by France's refusal to allow Israel to take delivery of the arms she had ordered and paid for. Or, again, he may have been inspired by memories of two articles on the arrest and torture of Communists in the United Arab Republic which *Les Temps Modernes* had published in 1960 and 1961.[18] What is certain is that Sartre was much more capable, in the 1960s, of adopting a balanced attitude towards the Arab-Israeli conflict than he was of taking a rational view of any aspect of American policy. In August 1966 *Les Temps Modernes* published a leading article entitled *'Capitulation ou Contre-escalade'*. In it, they urged Russia to give a clear warning to the United States that the next American escalation of the Vietnam war would meet with an immediate Russian military response. A little Russian brinkmanship, for *Les Temps Modernes*, was the only way to bring America to her senses, and Kossygin had a greater right to say 'I am a citizen of Hanoi' than Kennedy ever had to declare 'Ich bin ein Berliner'.

ii

In the late 1960s, Sartre's detestation of what he had already called 'that hell of misery and blood known as "The Free World" '[19] reached a new peak. In April 1968, in a speech which he gave at a meeting organized in Paris on behalf of the Black Power movement, he declared that it was 'the same aggressive force which holds down thirty million Vietnamese as well as twenty million Negroes in the USA', and went on to suggest, with every sign of approval, that the 'other Vietnams' demanded by Che Guevara might well be starting up at home in America even now.[20] Not until the student revolt of May 1968 did Sartre show any real enthusiasm for French politics. Violence, he declared, was the only way left open for the students who had not yet become part of the system established by their fathers to protest effectively against it. In our 'flabby Western societies' (*nos pays occidentaux avachis*) students were 'the sole left-wing force of contestation', and left-wing violence itself only the reply to the permanent violence which capitalist society exercised against all its members. To judge from even the most neutral press reports, the special French riot police did act in a peculiarly brutal manner when trying to control the student revolt of May 1968, and this was certainly not the only time that what Sartre called 'this collection of uniformed riff-raff known as the forces of order' (*ce ramassis en uniforme qu'on appelle des forces de l'ordre*) has shown how violent the class war can be in France.[21]

Sartre's enthusiasm for the student rebellion carried him to the point where he interviewed Daniel Cohn-Bendit in a style that seemed to acknowledge that a sixty-year-old philosopher had everything to learn from an undergraduate.[22] On 20 May 1968 he came to the Sorbonne and made a speech which expressed full support for the physical occupation of the university buildings by the students, and encouraged them to destroy the university as an institution under its present form. The rue le Goff, where Sartre spent his detested childhood, is within a few minutes walk of the Sorbonne, and the revenge which he seemed about to take on the academic society which his grandfather had taught him to treat with such reverence must have seemed particularly sweet. But like the other great periods of hope which Sartre once said that he had experienced – the Popular Front of 1936, the Liberation of France in 1944, the Peace Congress in Vienna in 1952[23] – the student revolt of 1968 again made no permanent contribution to the cause of socialism. When they came out on strike the workers appeared to be supporting the students, but once they had been given large pay rises, the Communist party and the Communist dominated Confédération Générale du Travail lost interest in the movement. In 1969 Sartre put his name to a pamphlet entitled '*Les Communistes ont Peur de la Révolution*', in which he accused the French Communist Party of effectively supporting the *status quo* in France, and not since 1956 has he seemed so critical of official Communist policy. The Russian invasion of Czechoslavakia in August 1968 led him to make a number of protests, and particularly to claim, in his preface to André Liehm's *Trois Générations* in 1970, that the French bourgeoisie was quite pleased with this damper put on '*le printemps de Prague*'. The creation of 'a holy alliance which will maintain Order everywhere' is now, in Sartre's view, the aim of those in power both in the East and in the West, and he sees only one way of ending this state of affairs. 'The machine will not be repaired,' he wrote in his preface to Liehm's book. 'The peoples of the world must seize hold of it and throw it on to the rubbish heap.'[24]

It is in this context that we must see Sartre's readiness to take on, in April 1970, the editorship of the Maoist *La Voix du Peuple*. The two previous editors had been put into prison for incitement to theft, looting, arson and murder, and Sartre announced his determination to prevent the government from effectively banning the paper, as it had tried to ban *Les Temps Modernes* during the Algerian war, by seizing every issue the moment it came out. If the government decided to arrest him, he declared, it would not be able to prevent his trial from becoming a political one. On 29 June he did succeed, very briefly, in getting himself taken into custody for three hours when he insisted on selling the paper in the street after the police had told him to stop. However, he was not brought to trial, and François Mauriac was able to depart this life with a last, decisive hit in his long duel with the man who had insulted him over thirty years earlier. 'Sartre's thirst for martyrdom,' he said, 'isn't enough to put somebody so incurably inoffensive in prison.'[25] Nevertheless, not everyone took the same view of Sartre's support for the most violent political movement ever to appear even in France. In the New Society so dramatically promised by the Prime Minister, Monsieur Chaban-Delmas in September 1969, wrote Raymond Barillon in *Le Monde* in May 1970, the fact remains that one can still find, six months later, a magistrate with nine thousand reports on juvenile delinquents to deal with, but unable to make any progress with his work because the government will not pay for him to have a secretary.[26] It is perhaps inevitable, if official French society is so stagnant, that the rebels it produces should show such despair in normal democratic methods.

For all his political activity during the last decade, Sartre has not ceased to work on his projected study of Flaubert. In May 1966, this was already reported as having attained the dimensions of six thousand manuscript pages,[27] and it will obviously be the longest book ever written about any author. In 1964, Sartre explained that he was so interested in Flaubert because he was the precise opposite of what he was himself, and his obsession with him also has strong personal origins. When he was a child, he read and re-read the closing pages of *Madame Bovary* until he knew them virtually by heart, and if he mentions Flaubert so frequently in his works, from *Qu'est-ce que la Littérature?* to *La Critique de la Raison Dialectique*, it is perhaps because he is still trying to exorcise his childhood. Michel Antoine Burnier, in *Les Existentialistes et la Politique*, also makes the interesting suggestion that Sartre's obsession with Flaubert stems from a kind of envy: Flaubert was a bourgeois through and through, and could attack his own class without ever running the risk of ceasing to belong to it; ideally, Sartre would like to have the same relationship with the proletariat, but knows that his birth and education will always prevent him from attaining it.[28] There is also another possible political reason for Sartre's fascination with the man whom he remembers, from the physical appearance of the books in his grandfather's study, as a 'small, clothbound, odourless creature, dotted with freckles'.[29] It is that he cannot bring himself, emotionally, to believe that French society has really changed since the end of the nineteenth century. His use of the word 'bourgeois' is certainly as far-reaching and uncritical as Flaubert's own, while the argument in *Les Communistes et la Paix* and *Saint Genet, Comédien et Martyr* is based on the presupposition that the men who ordered the massacres of the *Communards* or who supported the condemnation of Captain Dreyfus are still, spiritually and intellectually, in power in France. The fact that France was the last major European nation to lose her colonies, and then only after the bitterest resistance, tends to support this view, and it was a cliché of left-wing thought in the years immediately after de Gaulle's return to power in 1958 that the Fifth Republic was nothing but the Second Empire writ small.

Once again, however, it is Sartre himself who provides the most telling argument for anyone wishing to accuse him of being so fixated on the nineteenth century that he cannot free himself of Flaubert's ghost. Discussing the literary ideal instilled into him by Charles Schweitzer, he writes: 'This, it appears, explains the unchanging routine of peasant life. The fathers go off to the fields, leaving the children in the hands of the grandparents.'[30] It is precisely because the vision of society which Sartre received in his childhood came from a man born in the middle of the nineteenth century that he sees the social world in such a peculiar way. Like the other existentialist thinkers, like Pascal or Kierkegaard, his views become more and not less extreme as he grows older. Yet although, in his own submission, the root lies in his childhood, he still considers himself to be not a writer who expresses what no one else has said before, but one who 'writes what everybody thinks because he is like everybody else'.[31]

iii

It is perhaps in this respect that Sartre, for all his sympathy for Marxism, remains so thoroughly existentialist a thinker. When he writes that the Other 'perpetually lives his facticity in nausea as a non-positional apprehension of a contingency that he is'[32] he is not suggesting a possible way in which we might look at our own experience. He is telling us what life is like, just as Pascal is when he describes the natural state of man as 'inconstance, ennui, inquiétude'. Similarly, when he states that the worker's son 'feels in his flesh the very contingency of the weed',[33] and contrasts this intuition of the world's absurdity with the certainty that the bourgeois has of existing 'by divine right', he is not proposing a possible method of analysing what lies at the basis of different social attitudes. He is stating a fact, just as Kierkegaard is when he talks about the 'infinite and qualitative difference between God and Man'.

In his early work, especially in his study of the imagination, the statements which Sartre makes are supported by the same kind of rational, analytical approach which characterizes traditional English philosophy. In particular, his account of how the experiences of choice and action require the mind to possess certain qualities is extremely convincing. The problem arises when he moves away from analysis to apparently gratuitous affirmation – 'To be a man is to aspire to be God' ('Etre homme, c'est tendre à être Dieu')[34] – and still maintains that his argument depends upon evidence which everyone must find equally overwhelming. This is surely what he means when he writes that 'it is enough to open one's eyes and interrogate in all naïvety the reality of man-in-the-world',[35] and it is then that the temptation to fall back on the pose of being a 'plain man' becomes irresistible. Sartre's 'naive interrogation' may tell him that what he desires when making love is to 'feel his body open out to the point where he feels sick' ('sentir son corps s'épanouir jusqu'à la nausée');[36] but mine gives a different reply.

It is this objection which has always lain at the basis of the view that Sartre the imaginative writer is much better than Sartre the philosopher. That this view is only partly true can best be seen in *L'Imaginaire* or part IV, chapter I of *L'Etre et le Néant*. This is philosophical writing at the highest level, and the same thing is true of sections of *La Critique de la Raison Dialectique*. Moreover, there is one passage here that is peculiarly appropriate to the effect which Sartre's work has on some of his more hostile critics. When I hear a political broadcast with which I disagree, argues Sartre, I am annoyed less by its actual contents – for I, after all, know how to refute this pernicious nonsense – than by the effect which I realize it might have on an uncommitted but easily influenced listener.[37] The censors and moral theologians who placed Sartre's work on the Index were acting in accordance with this analysis, and the more violent the insults directed against him, the greater the implicit acknowledgment of Sartre's persuasiveness as a writer. A man whom Father Peter Dempsey, in a book published *cum approbatio ecclesiae*, can call a 'neurotic genius' who had 'rationalized his complexes' by writing books, or whom Gabriel Marcel can describe as a 'systematic blasphemer who has disseminated about him the most pernicious lessons and most poisonous advice ever poured out for the young by an acknowledged corrupter'[38] cannot be wholly bad. It is not difficult to see why apologists for systems which claim to possess absolute truth should be annoyed by Sartre. Even if Christians or Marxists are unmoved by the assertion that viscosity is the 'ontological expression of the whole world',[39] they cannot retain their original faith once they see the force of Sartre's argument that it is we who are free to create moral or political values by our actions, and not these values which create an obligation for us to act in one way rather than another.

It may well be nihilistic to argue that no moral law can be binding on me unless I personally choose to accept, by the acts I perform, the value system on which it is based. But it is a legitimate conclusion to draw from Sartre's vision of human freedom, and there is a sense in which his supporters are quite right when they attribute much of the opposition to his ideas to a kind of bad faith which makes people reluctant to acknowledge their freedom because they are afraid of it. Sartre's definition of his own brand of existentialism as an attempt to draw all the consequences from a consistently atheist position is applicable to every book that he has written, especially if atheism is taken in the broadest sense: the rejection of any philosophy which declares certain truths to be beyond question. The agnosticism which can, in this respect, be attributed to him is admittedly of a rather unusual kind. Unlike most people who reject absolute creeds, he holds no particular brief for tolerance. In fact, he goes so far as to argue, in *L'Etre et le Néant*, that all it does is compel the other person to live in a tolerant world.[40] This anticipation, in 1943, of the attack on the 'repressive tolerance' of Western society described in *The One-Dimensional Man* is particularly interesting in the light of the attitude which Sartre later adopted to the supposedly 'Marcuse-inspired' student revolt of May 1968.

Although Sartre once declared that he was 'incompetent on the technical plane of political action',[41] he appears to have had no real hesitation in joining that school of political thinkers which insists so much on the reality of conflict that it is not interested in any kind of society where people are allowed to mind their own business. He is attracted by the formal liberties of bourgeois society only in so far as they offer weapons by which this society might be destroyed, and it could be argued that here is a fundamental contradiction between the first and second parts of his career. The importance which he places on liberty when he is writing as a philosopher is difficult to reconcile with the increasingly left-wing bias of his political opinions, and especially so with his enthusiasm for those régimes which totally reject the Western democratic tradition. But at least he does not blink the fact that the extreme left has now completely parted company with the values of tolerance and intellectual freedom which were associated with it in the nineteenth century; while his cult of violence also suggests that he does not greatly mind if the respect for human life, again traditionally supposed to distinguish the left from the right, has now vanished from its ideology. He began his career by concentrating on what is perhaps the most private aspect of personal life, the way our imagination works. Now that he has become almost exclusively a political thinker, both the interest in people which showed itself in his novels and the concern for the niceties of philosophical enquiry which inspired his early essays seem to have disappeared.

Everything which Sartre has said about his own career implies regret that he came to politics so late. In 1955, he described himself as discovering, in 1939, that he had been mistaken in the meaning he had been giving to his life,[42] and Simone de Beauvoir's autobiography is shot through with regret that she and Sartre did not commit themselves earlier to the cause of the left. In fact, during the 1930s, Sartre did not even vote, and his attitude was one of scathing but anarchical contempt for all form of organized social existence. Had he committed himself earlier, it is at least conceivable that his political attitudes in both the fifties and the sixties would have been less determinedly left-wing. He might not have followed the example of an Orwell, a Malraux or a Koestler, who all came back from the Spanish Civil War convinced that fascism and Communism were both equally pernicious. But he would perhaps have assuaged the feelings of guilt which appear to have made him, in the last twenty years, run faster and faster in an attempt to catch up with something which he ought to have done when the issues were clear-cut and the Hun, so to speak, was at the gate. Like Pascal forsaking mathematics for religion, Sartre abandons literature and disinterested philosophical enquiry for politics. But whereas Pascal's rejection of science gave us the *Pensées*, Sartre's realization that literature has no value in a world where children die of hunger has so far produced only a large number of interviews in a left-wing weekly review.

Unlike Sartre's formal philosophical works, his novels and plays are, by the very nature of fiction, suggestions as to how we might look at our own experience, not attempts to impose a particular world view on us. It is not necessary, to appreciate Antoine Roquentin's nausea or Frantz von Gerlach's obsession with the future, to accept all the ideas in *L'Etre et le Néant* or *La Critique de la Raison Dialectique*. *La Nausée* and *Les Séquestrés d'Altona* carry their own world with them, just as do *L'Assommoir* and *The Brothers Karamazov*, and it has never been argued that only those who accept Zola's biological determinism can appreciate the first or that the second is incomprehensible to anyone hostile to the more reactionary views of the Greek Orthodox Church. We may also, if our political or philosophical views incline us that way, find *Les Mains Sales* a very convincing account of a certain political dilemma, but we do not need to have these views to appreciate it as a play. Such a pragmatic, piecemeal approach to his work would horrify Sartre himself, for he insists in *Saint Genet, Comédien et Martyr* that no distinctions can be made between the aesthetic qualities of a work and its moral or philosophical implications. It is nevertheless

fully consistent with Sartre's own view that the mind is always
free to detach itself from its immediate surroundings, and is also
the only way in which we can avoid the intellectual dishonesty
involved in accepting a philosophy as true in order to appreciate
the literature which it has inspired. It would nevertheless be
wrong to end this introduction to Sartre's work with the
impression that one has to search hard for the worthwhile ideas
which he expresses, or that these are merely thrown off accidentally
in the course of a fundamentally misguided account of human
experience. Towards the end of *Saint Genet* he remarks that
'optimism does not consist of saying that man is happy or that
he can be, but that he does not suffer for nothing'.[43] The theme
that links *Les Mots* and *L'Etre et le Néant* is that man's most
fundamental need is to make sense of his own experience. Sartre
himself did this when he chose to be a writer, and all the
characters in his work strive in their different ways to give a
coherent pattern to their lives.

Bibliography
Notes and references

Except when otherwise stated, all Sartre's works are quoted in
the standard Gallimard edition. By far the most useful book on
Sartre is Michel Contat and Michel Rybalka, *Les Ecrits de Sartre*
(Gallimard 1970). This gives a good summary of the main events
in his life, a brief analysis of each one of his books, an account of
the most important articles he has published, and an indication
of what he has said in his many interviews to the press. The most
balanced and perceptive studies of Sartre's work and ideas have,
however, all been published in English: Iris Murdoch's
Sartre, Romantic Rationalist, Bowes and Bowes, 1953; Maurice
Cranston's *Sartre*, Oliver and Boyd, Edinburgh 1962; Mary
Warnock's *Sartre*, Home University Library, 1965. The only
English critics of Sartre's work to have met with his formal approval,
however, are R. D. Laing and D. G. Cooper. Their study
Reason and Violence: a Decade in Sartre's Philosophy, Tavistock
Publications, 1964, has an enthusiastic foreword by Sartre, praising
them for having understood and presented his ideas very clearly.
The book is invaluable as a summary of the argument in *Saint
Genet, Comédien et Martyr* and *La Critique de la Raison Dialectique*.
The best book on any aspect of Sartre's work is Joseph P. Fell,
III *Emotion in the Thought of Sartre* (Columbia University Press,
1965). Francis Jeanson's *Sartre par Lui-même*, originally
published in 1956, was revised in 1969.

Novels
La Nausée Gallimard. 1939. Re-published in the Édition
    Pourpre series and in the 'Livre de Poche'.
Les Chemins de la Liberté:
I. *L'Age de Raison* Gallimard. 1945.
II. *Le Sursis* Gallimard. 1945.
III. *La Mort dans l'Ame* Gallimard. 1949.
Extracts of the fourth volume *La Dernière Chance* appeared
    under the title of '*Drôle d'Amitié*' in *Les Temps Modernes*,
    November and December 1949.
Le Mur Gallimard. 1939. Re-published in the 'Livre de Poche'
    series.

Plays

Les Mouches Gallimard. 1943. Re-published in *Théâtre*. Gallimard
   1947.
Huis Clos, Morts sans Sépulture, La Putain Respectueuse
   Published in *Théâtre*. 1947.
Les Mains Sales Gallimard. 1948. Re-published in the Édition
   Pourpre series.
Le Diable et le Bon Dieu Gallimard. 1951.
Kean, ou Désordre et Génie Adapted from Alexandre Dumas.
   Gallimard. 1954.
Nekrassov Gallimard. 1956.
Les Séquestrés d'Altona Gallimard. 1960.
Les Troyennes Gallimard. 1965.

Collected Essays

Situations I Gallimard. 1947. (On Faulkner, Dos Passos, Paul
   Nizan, Husserl, Mauriac, Nabokov, Denis de Rougement,
   Giraudoux, Camus, Blanchot, Bataille, Parain, Renard,
   Descartes.) These essays date from between 1938 and 1946.

Situations II Gallimard. 1948. Présentation des Temps Modernes,
   La Nationalisation de la Littérature, Qu'est-ce que la Littérature?

Situations III Gallimard. 1949. La Répulbique du Silence,
   Paris sous l'Occupation, Qu'est-ce qu'un Collaborateur? La
   Fin de la Guerre, Individualisme et Conformisme aux
   États-Unis, Villes d'Amérique, Matérialisme et Révolution,
   Orphée Noir, La Recherche de l'absolu, Les Mobiles de
   Calder.

Situations IV Portraits Gallimard. 1964. Portrait d'un inconnu,
   L'Artiste et sa conscience, Des rats et des hommes, Gide
   vivant, Réponse à Albert Camus, Albert Camus, Paul Nizan,
   Merleau-Ponty, Le séquestré de Venise, Les peintures
   de Giacometti, Le peintre sans privilèges, Masson, Doigts
   et non-doignts, Un parterre de capucines, Venise, de ma
   fenêtre.

Situations V Colonialisme et Néo-colonialisme, Gallimard. 1964. '*D'une Chine à l'autre*, Le colonialisme est un système, '*Portrait du colonisé*' précédé du '*Portrait du colonisateur*', '*Vous êtes formidables*', '*Nous sommes tous des assassins*', Une victoire, '*Le Prétendant*', La Constitution du mépris, Les grenouilles qui demandent un roi, L'analyse du Référendum, Les Somnambules, '*Les Damnés de la terre*', La pensée politique de Patrice Lumumba.

Situations VI Gallimard. 1964. Portrait de l'aventurier, Faux savants ou faux lièvres, Sommes-nous en démocratie? 'La fin de l'espoir', Les communistes la paix.

Situations VII Gallimard. 1965. Résponse à Claude Lefort, Opération 'Kanapa', Le réformisme et les fétiches, Réponse à Pierre Naville, Le fantôme de Staline, Quand la police frappe les trois coups . . . La démilitarisation de la culture, Discussion sur la critique à propos de 'L'Enfance d'Ivan'.

General and Political Studies

Réflexions sur la Question Juive Éditions Morihien. 1946 Republished by Gallimard. 1954
Baudelaire Gallimard. 1947
Entretiens sur la Politique Gallimard. 1949.
Saint Genet, Comédien et Martyr Gallimard. 1952.
L'Affaire Henri Martin Gallimard. 1953. Commentary by Sartre on texts by a number of other writers.

Sartre on Cuba Ballantine Books, New York. 1961.
Four long extracts of the promised essay on Flaubert, *L'Idiot de la Famille,* have appeared in *Les Temps Modernes*: *La Conscience de Classe chez Flaubert*, Parts I and II in May and June 1966; '*Du Poète à l'Artiste*', Parts I and II, August and September 1966.
Another, shorter essay, *Père et Fils*, appeared in Hachette's *Livres de France*, January number, 1966. This also contains a useful bibliography of Sartre's works.

Autobiography
Les Mots Gallimard. 1964.

Philosophical Works
L'Imagination Presses Universitaires de France. 1936.
Esquisse d'une Théorie des Emotions Herman et Cie. 1939.
L'Imaginaire: Psychologie Phénoménologique de l'Imagination.
   Gallimard. 1940.
L'Etre et le Néant : Essai d'ontologie phénoménologique Gallimard.
   1943.
L'Existentialisme est un Humanisme Nagel. 1946.
La Critique de la Raison Dialectique Gallimard. 1960.
Marxisme et Existentialisme. Controverse sur la Dialectique.
   (With others.) Plon. 1962

Notes and references

Abbreviations
The following Abbreviations are used in the notes:
CRD – *La Critique de la Raison Dialectique*; DBD – *Le Diable et le Bon Dieu*; EN – *L'Etre et le Néant*; AR – *L'Age de Raison*; Mo – *Les Mots*; Nau – *La Nausée*; SdA – *Les Séquestrés d'Altona*; SGCM - St. Genet, Comedien at Martyr; *Sit*. I, II, III, etc. – *Situations I, II, III, etc.*

I have kept the notes to a minimum, and should be happy to supplement them if any reader would care to write to me privately.

Notes to Chapter 1
1. Mo 13
2. Mo 3. See also Albert Schweitzer, *My Life and Thought*, Allen and Unwin, 1968, p. 31, in which Charles Schweitzer is referred to as 'a linguist who had made a name for himself by his efforts to improve the teaching of modern languages'
3. See *L'Existentialisme est un Humanisme*, Nagel, Paris, 1951, p. 94. The text of a lecture given at the Club Maintenant on 29 October 1945
4. *Réflexions sur la Question Juive*, p. 82
5. *Présentation des 'Temps Modernes'*, *Sit*. II, p. 19
6. Interview in *Le Figaro littéraire*, 30.6.51.
7. SGCM 55
8. *Le Monde*, 18.4.64. Interview with Jacqueline Piatier. Fɩr a full translation, see *Encounter*, June 1964.
9. *Le Monde*, 18.4.64.
10. Nau 221
11. Nau 142
12. EN 98
13. EN 641–63
14. SGCM 55
15. *Flaubert*, Livres de France, Hachette, January 1966, p. 22
16. EN 474 and 607. See also *Sit*. II, p. 247; SG 80
17. *Baudelaire*, p. 56
18. *Le Monde*. 18.4.64.
19. *The New Left Review*, No. 58, November–December 1969, p. 66

Notes to Chapter 2

1. Jeanson, *Sartre par Lui-même*. Editions du Seuil, Paris 1956, p. 116
2. *Sit.* IV, pp. 160–1
3. *Nouvel Observateur*, 19.6.68. 'Les Bastilles de Raymond Aron'
4. *Mémoires d'une Jeune Fille Rangée*, p. 310
5. *Force de L'Age*, p. 18. *Sit.* II, p. 16 and 195–6
6. *Le Monde*, 18.4.64; Mo. 211
7. *Mémoires d'une Jeune Fille Rangée*, p. 340; Nau 16, 48
8. See the *Observer*, 23.2.63 and *France-Observateur*, 28.2.63
9. *Force de l'Age*, p. 134; EN etc: 101–3
10. EN, 535–7
11. I am indebted to my friend and colleague Professor Garnet Rees, of the University of Hull, for this independent view of Sartre's personality in the thirties.
12. Marc Beigbeder, *L'Homme Sartre*, Paris, Bordas, 1947 contains a photograph of the programme for *A l'ombre des vieilles billes en fleurs*; Contat and Rybalka, p. 23
13. *Sit.* IV, p. 164
14. *Force des Choses*, p. 251
15. The text of *La Légende de la Vérité* is given in Contat and Rybalka, pp. 531–45
16. AR, 82
17. The text of this speech is in Contat and Rybalka, pp. 546–52.
18. *Nouvel Observateur*, 19.6.68.
19. *Les Nouvelles Littéraires*, 3.12.38.
20. *Force de l'Age*, p.151 (London), p. 141 (Stracey), p. 149 (Cynara).
21. *France-Observateur*, 2.3.61.
22. See p. 3 of Forrest Williams's translation of *L'Imagination: Imagination, a psychological critique*, Ann Arbor, 1962
23. *The Concept of Mind*, University Paperbacks, 1962 p. 254
24. This article was re-published in 1965 in the Librairie Philosophique Vrin with an excellent set of notes by Sylvie Le Bon.
25. *L'Imaginaire*, p. 227
26. EN, 697
27. *L'Imaginaire*, p. 122
28. *L'Imaginaire*, p. 189–90
29. *L'Imaginaire*, p. 161 and p. 189
30. *La Force de l'Age*, p. 228
31. *Theatre Arts*, July 1946. *Forgers of Myths. The new playwrights of France*, pp. 324–35
32. *Esquisse d'une théorie des Emotions*. Hermann et Cie., Paris, 1948 p. 42
33. *L'Imaginaire*, p. 245

Notes to Chapter 3

1. See Marcel Arland in *La Nouvelle Revue Française*, July 1938, pp. 126–38; *Mercure de France*, 15.7.38; Edmond Jaloux, *Les Nouvelles Littéraires*, 18.6.38.
2. EN 404
3. *Théâtre*, 1947, p. 102
4. EN 409; see *Club*, May 1954
5. AR 53; Nau. 163
6. See *La Force de l'Age*, pp. 304–6; and G. H. Bauer's excellent study *Sartre and the Artist*, University of Chicago Press, 1969.
7. Nau 169
8. EN 708
9. Nau 198
10. *A Treatise of Human Nature*, Part IV, Section XIV. Quoted by Isaiah Berlin, *The Age of Enlightenment*, N.A.L., p. 214
11. *Punch*, 7.12.49. See also Panther paperbacks.
12. EN 615–42
13. *Force de l'Age*, p. 39
14. *L'Imaginaire*, pp. 189–90
15. SdA. 146
16. *Second Manifeste du Surréalisme*, 1930.
17. EN 471–73
18. René Varin. *L'Erotisme dans la Littérature Contemporaine*, Editions de la Pensée Moderne, Paris, 1953. Sartre is included in the section illustrating realistic eroticism.
19. *Le Mur*, p. 119
20. *Le Mur*, p. 124
21. EN 93
22. *Le Mur*, 122 and 124; AR 23; but in view of the plot of AR, Mathieu's reply to Irene in *Le Sursis*, p. 300, is inexplicable; *Mort dans l'âme*, p. 150; cf. also Simone de Beauvoir, in *Force de l'Age*, p. 101; and, more amusingly, *Force des Choses*, p. 104
23. *Le Mur*, p. 220
24. *Réflexions*, p. 65
25. *Réflexions*, p. 37
26. Mo 72
27. *Le Sursis*, p. 47
28. *Le Figaro*, 26.6.51. Sartre's article, *Monsieur François Mauriac et la Liberté*, first appeared in the *Nouvelle Revue Française* in February 1939 and was widely discussed. In 1969, Mauriac explained his long silence as a novelist partly by reference to Sartre's article. (*France-Soir*, 28.2.69)
29. *Sit.* I, p. 295
30. *Sit.* I, p. 196
31. *Sit.* I, p. 137

150   SARTRE

Notes to Chapter 4

1. *Sit*, IV, 190, footnote; see also Brunet's comments in *Drôle d'Amitié, Les Temps Modernes*, November 1949, p. 776
2. *Force de l'Age*, p. 440; realized liberty behind barbed wire, *Les Nouvelles Littéraire*, 1.2.51.
3. *Le Figaro Littéraire*, 26.3.60; *Bariona* is now available in Contat and Rybalka, pp. 565–633. Since 1952 a small number of copies had been available to research students personally recommended to Sartre.
4. Contat and Rybalka, pp. 373–5
5. *Force de l'Age*, p. 493
6. *Force de l'Age*, p. 513–4; cf. also *Sit*. VI. 166
7. *France Observateur*, 29.10.64.
8. Cf. *Le Petit Parisien*, 5.6.43; *La Gerbe*, 17.6.43.
9. *Carrefour*, 9.9.44.
10. *Théâtre*, 108
11. *Théâtre*, 102
12. EN 431 and 321
13. Jacques Lemarchand, *Combat*, 26.9.46.
14. *Sit*. II, 26–7
15. EN 145
16. Alexandre Astruc. *Poésie*, 44, p. 193
17. EN 713
18. EN 45
19. EN 75
20. EN 270
21. EN 97
22. EN 165
23. EN 656
24. EN 658
25. EN 253
26. SGCM 132
27. EN 671
28. EN 705
29. EN 705
30. EN 653–4
31. EN 481 and 349
32. EN 721
33. EN 721–2
34. *Sit*. III, p. 12
35. *Descriptions Critiques*, Gallimard, 1949, p. 165. The article was written in 1946, and Roy had been a Communist since 1943. He left the Party in 1956
36. *Force des Choses*, p. 128
37. *Les Nouvelles Littéraires*, 21.11.46; *Libération*, 16.7.54.
38. Cf. *Neuphilologische Mitteilungen*, 1950, pp. 128–30
39. *France-Dimanche*, 17.11.46.

40. *Sit.* II, p. 29
41. Jeanson, op. cit.
42. *The Times*, 1.11.48; Fadeiev, quoted by *Les Temps Modernes*, October 1948, p. 757

Notes to Chapter 5
 1. *Sit.* II, 280, 285
 2. *Sit.* II, 140–1
 3. *Sit.* II, 122
 4. Contat and Rybalka, p. 122. Quoted from *Les Temps Modernes*, June 1948
 5. *Sit.* II, 260
 6. Mo 148
 7. Le Monde, 18.4.64; *Encounter*, June 1964, p. 61
 8. *Sit.* II, 272
 9. *Sit.* II, 272
10. *Sit,* II, 196; paradox – *Sit.* II, 275–6
11. *Sit.* II, 70
12. *Sit.* II, 20
13. *Sit.* II, 112–13
14. *L'Express*, 3.3.60.
15. *Mercure de France*, 1.7.48.
16. *Le Sursis*, p. 335
17. Published in Hillel, *Organe de l'Union Mondiale des Etudiants Juifs*, January 1947, p. 29. The text is in Contat and Rybalka, pp. 141–2. *Portrait de l'Anti-sémite* was published in *Les Temps Modernes*, December 1945, pp. 442–470. It coincides with the first part of the standard Gallimard edition of the *Réflexions sur la Question Juive*.
18. *Réflexions*, 62
19. Contat and Rybalka, p. 140. Quotation from an interview given to *Alhamishar* in 1966 and translated in *New Outlook*, May, 1966, pp. 8–11
20. See Sidney Hook's review of the English translation, '*Anti-semite and Jew,*' in *Partisan Review*, April 1949, pp. 463–82
21. *Nouvel Observateur*, 18.3.67.
22. *Sit.* II, 27 and 237. *Baudelaire,* 56–7
23. *Sit.* II, 112; both for anti-semitism and American Negro
24. See advertisement in *Les Nouvelles Littéraires*, 30.12.39; Contat and Rybalka, p. 114
25. *Sursis*, 340
26. *Le Figaro Littéraire*, 26.6.51.
27. See interview in *Paru,* with Christian Grisoli, December 1945, pp. 5–10
28. *Le Sursis*, 107–8
29. *Le Sursis*, 37–40; his prediction, AR, 310

30. AR 310
31. AR 33, 69, 97 and 202, 195. On p. 197 of *La Force des Choses* Simone de Beauvoir remarks that Sartre had difficulty communicating with Nelson Algren because he didn't speak English.
32. *La Force des Choses*, pp. 213–15
33. *Sursis*, 257–8. For Sartre's acknowledgment of his debt to Dos Passos, see his 'American novelists in French Eyes', *Atlantic Monthly*, August 1946 pp. 114–18
34. *Théâtre*, 102

Notes to Chapter 6

1. *L'Humanité*, 7.4.48; Contat and Rybalka, p. 487
2. Contat and Rybalka p. 181 and 183. For Sartre's protests against staging *Les Mains Sales*, see *Le Monde* 19.11.52 and the reports of his press conference on 25.9.54.
3. Contat and Rybalka, p. 183
4. *Les Temps Modernes*, November 1949, p. 799
5. *Opéra*, 5.1.49; *Partisan Review*, April 1949, pp. 407–11; *La Force des Choses*, p. 186
6. *L'Aurore*, 25.6.57; Thierry Maulnier's review was printed in *Le Spectateur*, 6.4.48. He is normally hostile to Sartre's political ideas and wrote a long attack on *L'Affaire Henri Martin* in the right-wing *La Table Ronde*, in December 1953, pp. 29–39, accusing Sartre of wishing to add a third to the other two great catastrophes of French history: the surrender of Canada to the English in 1763; the sale of Louisiana to the United States in 1803
7. Dussane, *Notes de Théâtre*, Lyon, 1951, p. 158; the English translation was published by Hamish Hamilton 1949.
8. EN 583–4
9. *Force des Choses*, 194
10. *Sit.* III, 225 and 172
11. *Paris-Match*, 2.5.70; *Les Nouvelles Littéraires*, 20.12.51.
12. MS 205
13. *Force de l'Age*, 82–3
14. MS 131; Contat and Rybalka, p. 183, quoting an interview which Sartre gave in 1964 and in which he said that Hoederer was the kind of person he would have liked to be if he had been a revolutionary.
15. See *La Force des Choses*, pp. 140–224
16. *La Force des Choses*, 312
17. See Contat and Rybalka, 192. For all other details on the relationship between Sartre and Genet, together with an admirable discussion of Genet's work, see Richard Coe's *The Vision of Jean Genet*, Peter Owen, 1968.

18. Contat and Rybalka, pp. 242–3
19. SGCM 55: *Réflexions*, 84; for an 'inauthentic' Jew in Sartre's fiction, see *Le Sursis*, pp. 72–81; and for the origin of Monsieur Birmenschatz's view of his daughter (*Sursis*, p. 77), see *Réflexions*, 125
20. SGCM 56
21. SGCM 211
22. SGCM 548
23. SGCM 68
24. SGCM 463 and 389
25. SGCM 152
26. SGCM 231
27. *Nouvel Observateur*, 24.6.65.
28. *La Force des Choses*, pp. 261–2
29. Mo 213
30. *Sit.* VI, 1938. The articles *Les Communistes et la Paix* appeared in *Les Temps Modernes* in July 1952, October–November 1952, and April 1954.
31. *Les Temps Modernes*, August 1952. A full account of the circumstances of this quarrel, which arose out of an unfavourable review which Francis Jeanson gave of Camus's *L'Homme Révolté* in the May 1952 number of *Les Temps Modernes*, can be found in Contat and Rybalka, pp. 249–51.
32. *Le Figaro Littéraire*, 1.2.51.
33. Contat and Rybalka, p. 418. Based on a long article by Simone de Beauvoir, translated into English by Malcom Cowley and published in *Harper's Bazaar*, June 1946; Troisfontaines, Contat and Rybalka, pp. 144–5
34. *Force des Choses*, p. 27
35. *Force des Choses*, pp. 267, 378, 398
36. *Force des Choses*, p. 342

Notes to Chapter 7

1. This quarrel was sparked off by the publication of an article entitled *Sartre et le Néo-Bolchevisme* in Merleau-Ponty's *Les Aventures de la Dialectique*, Gallimard, 1955. Simone de Beauvoir replied to this criticism of *Les Communistes et la Paix* in an article entitled *Merleau-Ponty et le pseudo-Sartrisme*, published in *Les Temps Modernes* for June–July 1955 and reprinted in *Privilèges* in the same year. All the arguments used are highly recommended for gallophile insomniacs.
2. E-N. Dzenepely, *Les Temps Modernes*, December 1950, *Mac Arthur et l'Affaire de Corée*, pp. 961–1010; and February 1951, *Le 'Pearl Harbour' de Mac Arthur*, pp. 1361–1499. I. F. Stone, *La Guerre Fantôme*, August, 1951, pp. 209–43 and *La guerre comme politique*, pp. 460–82

3. *Sit.* VI, 105; for attack on Marshall Plan, see Pierre Uri, *Les Temps Modernes*, July 1948, *Une Stratégie Economique*, pp. 1–11. On Berlin, see *La Force des Choses*, p. 176 arguing that the Russian blockade in 1948 was a riposte to Western provocation in introducing the new currency into West Germany. For Sartre's view that the Germans were the '*ennemis séculaires*' (age-old enemies) of the French, see Contat and Rybalka, p. 249, quoting from *France-U.R.S.S. Magazine*, April 1955. For a view of the 1961 Berlin crisis that Sartre may have shared, see Heinz Abosch, *Le Crépuscule de Konrad Adenauer*, *Les Temps Modernes*, December 1961, pp. 737–51. It is not possible to discover what Sartre or *Les Temps Modernes* thought of the unilateral resumption of nuclear testing by the Soviet Union on 1 September 1961, because such matters, like the Russian attempt to install missiles in Cuba, are never mentioned.

4. *Force des Choses*, 280–1. *Les Temps Modernes* have since published a number of other articles by Guillemin, which taken together represent a consistently left-wing view of French history. See his *Origines de la Commune*, with Thiers as the villain, in 1955–9; his *L'Affaire pas Morte*, in November 1961; his *Genèse d'un paradis (de Thermidor à Louis-Philippe)*, July 1966, especially the sentence (pp. 139–40) 'En 1830 aboutit enfin cette longue mise en place, entamée depuis la fin du XVIII siècle, du système qui doit permettre l'exploitation forcenée de la substance française par le "petit nombre" dont parlait Voltaire'; and *Monsieur Louis Bonaparte*, January 1967. The book which so influenced Sartre in 1952 was *Le coup d'état du 2 décembre*.

5. *Sit.* IV, 249

6. *Sit.* VI, 86–7, 197, 279; *Le Mur*, p. 189

7. *Spain.*

8. The articles appeared between 15.7.54 and 20.7.54.

9. *New Statesman*, 3.12 55. He also told Pierre Heutges, of *L'Humanité*, that it was 'pure madness to imagine that there could be any reasons whatsoever for a divorce between these two countries', (1.11.55; quoted by Contat and Rybalka, p. 291)

10. Contat and Rybalka, p. 268 quote a long extract from the programme on sale at the Théâtre Sarah Bernhardt when *Kean* was produced. It appears from this that the play which Sartre adapted was not even by Dumas *fils*, but by a man called de Courcy.

11. *Kean*, 165–6; SGCM, 29

12. *Kean*, 165–6; *Les Mots*, 57–8, 92–3, 111

13. Jeanson, *Sartre par lui-même*, 1969 edition, p. 111

14. *L'Humanité*, 8.6.55.

15. *Paris-Presse L'Intransigeant*, 15.6.55.
15. *Sit.* VII, 236
17. *Sit.* VII, 237
18. The preface is reprinted in *Situations* VI, pp. 23–68. See pp. 39–40 for an argument comparable to the one put forward in *Le Fantôme de Staline*. In January 1950, *Les Temps Modernes* published a leading article entitled 'Les Jours de notre vie' condemning the use of forced labour camps in Russia. The article was actually written by Maurice Merleau-Ponty.
19. CRD 17
20. Contat and Rybalka, 310
21. CRD 28
22. Thus compare CRD 295–9 with *Sit.* VI, 325–33; CRD 714–5 with *Sit.* VI, 278–80; and CRD 725–6 with *Sit.* VI, 393–7.
23. CRD 269; for Sartre's two examples, see CRD, 269–43.

Notes to Chapter 8
1. Contat and Rybalka, p. 544
2. *Le Nouvel Observateur*, 1.4.65.
3. *Sit .V*, 28
4. CRD 675. The whole of this passage has strong resemblances to *Le Colonialisme est un Système*.
5. The text of *Une Victoire* is in *Situations V*, pp. 72–88
6. *Les Temps Modernes*, May–June 1958, pp. 147–8. Quoted by Antoine Burnier in *Les Existentialistes et la Politique*, p. 126
7. *Sit.* V, pp. 102–13. Originally in *L'Express*, 11.9.58.
8. SdA 213
9. See Dominique Fernandez in *La Nouvelle Revue Française* November 1959; Robert Benavoun, *Le Nouvel-Observateur* 21.11.63; François Périer, *Le Nouvel-Observateur*, 8.9.65.
10. *Sit.* V, 81; see also *Sit.* VII, 161
11. SGCM 549; see also Contat and Rybalka, p. 175
12. SdA 217
13. CRD 289–91
14. *New Left Review*, November–December 1969, p. 44
15. SdA 49
16. See also Madeleine Field's article *De 'La Critique de la raison dialectique' aux 'Séquestrés d'Altona'*. PMLA, December 1963, pp. 622–30. Sartre – Protestant conscience, *Paris-Journal*, 12.9.59; created in his own image, 103, cf. Genesis, I, 27: Prodigal Son, 143, cf. Luke, XV, 11–32; remaining awake, 93, cf. Matthew, XXVI, 41; parody of Last Supper, 188, cf. Luke XXII, 19–20
17. See Alfred Simon, *Esprit*, November 1959, p. 551
18. CRD 208
19. *France-Observateur*, 22.9.60.

20. *Nouvel Observateur*, 30.11.66.
21. Nos 166, 173, 174, 180 and 186 were all seized during this period
22. *Force des Choses*, p. 407
23. Cf. Burnier, op. cit. p. 152 and *La Force des Choses*, pp. 117–18 and 378
24. *Force des Choses*, pp. 272–3.
25. *Sit.* IV, p. 138
26. *Sit.* V, p. 243–4
27. *Sit.* V, 172
28. *Sit.* V, p. 183
29. In May 1970, *Les Temps Modernes* published the manifesto of the 'weathermen'.
30. Contat and Rybalka, pp. 454–5

Notes to Chapter 9
1. Mo 212
2. *Le Monde*, 18.4.64; *Preuves*, May 1964, pp. 72–4
3. *Le Monde*, 28.10.64.
4. *Nouvel Observateur*, 20.2.64.
5. *Nouvel Observateur*, 31.12.64.
6. *Le Monde*, 24.10.64.
7. *The Times*, 20.10.67; Sartre is always included in the list of Honorary graduates for the University of Leeds.
8. *Le Monde*, 24.10.64.
9. *La Force des Choses*, 333
10. *Le Monde*, 18.4.64.
11. *Bref. Journal du Théâtre National Populaire*, February 1965.
12. *Nouvel Observateur*, 1.4.65; David Grossvogel's reply, *Nouvel Observateur*, 8.4.65.
13. *Nouvel Observateur*, 30.11.66.
14. *Nouvel Observateur*, 26.4.67.
15. Mo 211
16. *Le Monde*, 24.10.64; *Nouvel Observateur*, 16.11.66; *Le Monde*, 14.8.66. Sartre has not, however, so far expressed an opinion on Northern Ireland.
17. *Le Monde*, 1.6.67; see also *Nouvel Observateur*, 14.6.67.
18. Abel Montasser, *La Répression anti-démocratique en Egypte*, *Les Temps Modernes*, July 1960 and July 1961; but see also Sartre's description of the late President Nasser as a 'prudent, judicious and far-sighted man'. *Le Monde*, 15.3.67.
19. *Nouvel Observateur*, 10.11.68.
20. Meeting held on 30.4.68. See Contat and Rybalka, p. 474.
21. A broadcast interview given on Radio-Luxembourg on 12.5.68 and duplicated for circulation by the students themselves. Cf. Contat and Rybalka, p. 463; *Nouvel Observateur*, 4.11.68.

22. Special number of *Le Nouvel Observateur*, 20.5.68.
23. *Lettres Françaises*, 1.1.53.
24. *Trois Générations*, Gallimard, collections *Témoins*, 1970. Sartre's preface is entitled '*Un socialisme qui venait du froid*'. Cf. p. XXXI
25. Cf. *The Times*, 30.6.70; and the *Observer*, 'Sayings of the Week', 26.7.70.
26. *Le Monde*, 29.4.70.
27. *Nouvel Observateur*, 18.5.66; Mo 42
28. Burnier, op. cit., p. 184–5
29. Mo 50
30. Mo 49
31. *The Listener*, 6 June 1957, p. 915. Interview with Olivier Todd.
32. EN 409
33. SGCM 240
34. EN 653–4
35. EN 38
36. EN 467
37. CRD 321
38. See Peter J. R. Dempsey, *The Psychology of Sartre*, Cork and O.U.P., 1950, p. 24; Gabriel Marcel, *Les Nouvelles Littéraires*, 29.10.64.
39. EN 698
40. EN 480
41. *Le Monde*, 1.6.55.
42. Ibid. See also *The Listener*, 6 June 1957, p. 915
43. SGCM 512–13

Selective Index

Alain (= Chartier, E.-A.) 25, 26
Algren, Nelson 94
Alleg, Henri 115–16, 119
Aron, Raymond 34, 39
Auden, W. H. 43, 75, 105

Baudelaire, Charles 20, 21, 24,
    51, 70, 80–1, 131
Beauvoir, Simone de 24, 26–7,
    28, 32, 48, 52, 65, 74–5, 84, 93,
    94, 95, 98, 107, 126–7, 132,
    141
Beethoven, Ludwig von 39, 44
Browning, Robert 63, 79

Calvin, John 14, 66
Camus, Albert 30, 58–9, 64, 81,
    91, 99
Chaplin, Charles 75
Cocteau, Jean 95, 113
Cohn-Bendit, Daniel 65, 136
Contat, Michel 25, 143
Cooper, R. M. 70, 143
Courteline, Georges 29
Corneille, Pierre 12, 39, 65
Cranston, Maurice 143

Descartes, René 25, 59
Dostoyevsky, Fyodor 37, 70, 84,
    141
Dos Passos, John 58, 84–5
Dowson, Ernest 33

El-Kaim, Arlette (Sartre's adopted
    daughter) 129

Fadeiev 76
Fanon, Franz 128–9
Faulkner, William 58
Fell, Joseph P. III 143
Flaubert, Gustave 17, 20, 70, 75,
    84, 110, 133, 137–8
Francis of Assisi, St. 22
Franco, General 47, 134
Freud, Sigmund 25, 55, 69–70,
    75

Genet, Jean 11, 20, 70, 94–7, 106,
    112, 120, 130
Gide, André 33, 62, 82, 131
Guevara, Che 65, 129, 135

Guillemin, Louise (grandmother
    to Sartre) 8, 9, 13
Guillemin, Henri (French his-
    torian) 103, 154

Hammarskjöld, Dag 128
Hegel, G. W. F. 110
Heidegger, Martin 15, 47
Hemingway, Ernest 48, 100
Hitler, Adolf 46, 121
Hume, David 46
Husserl, Edmund 29, 34–5
Huxley, Aldous 27

Ibsen, Henrik 35

Jaspers, Karl 15, 91
Jeanson, Francis 24, 99, 106,
    124–5, 143
Jolson, Al 28

Kafka, Franz 41
Kant, Emmanuel 32, 36, 37, 68,
    76, 133
Kierkegaard, Sören 14, 15, 72,
    79, 110, 138
Kipling, Rudyard 29, quoted 141
Knox, John 66

Laing, R. D. 70, 143
Lawrence, D. H. 47
Leeds, University of 132
Lloyd George 54
Locke, John 33

Malraux, André 48, 141
Mancy, M. (step-father to Sartre)
    24–5, 56, 75, 103
Marcel, Gabriel 74, 139
Marcuse, Herbert 140
Marx (brothers) 28
Marx, Karl 58–9, 72–3, 95,
    110–12
Maulnier, Thierry 90, 152
Mauriac, François 58–9, 83, 137
Merleau-Ponty, Maurice 62, 102
Mill, J. S. 50
Molière 77
Murdoch, Iris 143

Newman, Henry 66

Nietzsche 31, 41
Nizan, Paul 30, 127

Pascal, Blaise 15, 79, 138, 141
Punch 42, 47
Proust, Marcel 30, 41, 62

Racine, Jean 39
Rassemblement Démocratique
Révolutionnaire 91–2
Rousseau, Jean-Jacques 9, 78,
80
Roy, Claude 62, 74
Russell, Bertrand 9, 129, 133–4
Rybalka, Michel 25, 143
Ryle, Gilbert 34–5

Sartre, Jean-Baptiste 7, 9, 17, 18,
24
Sartre, Jean-Paul: works dis-
cussed:
Affaire Henri Martin, L' **112–13**
Age de Raison, L' **83–5**, 29,
31, 42, 47
Ange du Morbide, L' 30–1
Bariona **60–2**, 83, 106, 122
Baudelaire **80–1**, 20, 21
Chambre, La **48–9**, 10, 118,
119
Chemins de la Liberté, Les
41, **82–6**, 118
Colonialisme est un Système, Le
115–16
Communisme Jougoslave Depuis
Tito, Le (Preface to book by
Louis Delmas) 110
Communistes et la Paix, Les
103–5, 14, 111, 138
Communistes ont Peur de la
Revolution, Les 136
Critique de la Raison Dialec-
tique, La **110–12**, 84, 99, 115,
121, **123–4**, 126, 128, 137,
139, 141
Dernière Chance, La **85–6**, 89
Diable et le Bon Dieu, Le **97–
9**, 8, 65, 92, 119, 122, 124
Drôle d'Amitié 86, 96
Enfance d'un Chef, L' **54–7**,
25, 91, 104
Erostrate **51–2**
Esquisse d'une Théorie des Émo-
tions **38–9**, 49
Etre et le Néant, L' **66–73**, 18,
20, 29, 37, 41, 42, 46, 51, 52,
54, 55, 64, 75, 86, 91, 111,
121, 139, 140, 141, 142
Exigences Contradictoires, Nos
135

Fantôme de Staline, Le **108–
10**
Genocide, On 129
Huis Clos **64–6**, 10, 50, 61, 92,
99, 118, 119
Imaginaire, L' **35–40**, 41, 48–
9, 66, 139
Imagination, L' **34–5**, 31
Intimité **51–4**
Kean **105–7**, 119
Légende de la Vérité, La **30–1**,
33, 113
Mains Sales, Les **86–94**, 22,
57, 61, 99, 105, 109, 119, 120,
141
Matérialisme et Revolution 73,
92
Mort dans l'Ame, La 31, 60
Morts sans Sépulture 74, 116
Mots, Les **7–23**, 40, 42, 43, 70,
78, 98, 120, 121, **130–2**, 134,
142
Mouches, Les **62–4**, 42, 60,
100, 117, 122
Mur, Le **47–57**, 10, 60
Nausée, La **41–7**, 14, 27, 29,
49, 67, 83, 84, 120, 132, 141
Nekrassov **106–8**, 119
Putain respectueuse, La **74–5**
Qu'est-ce que la Littérature?
78–80, 21, 22, 26, 37, 81, 88,
92, 131, 137
Questions de Méthode **110–11**
Réflexions sur la Question Juive
56–7, **81–2**, 87, 129
Saint Genet, Comédien et
Martyr **94–7**, 8, 11, 14, 20,
71, 99, 106, 122, 130, 138, 141,
142
Séquestrés d'Altona, Les **117–
24**, 10, 17, 50, 81, 126, 127,
130, 141
Sursis, Le **83–5**
Transcendance de l'Ego, La
35, 68 (by implication), 91
Trois Générations (preface to
book by André Liehm) 136
Troyennes, Les **133**
Victoire, Une 116, 119
Sartre's ideas, attitudes and
experiences:
account of childhood **7–23**,
106, **130–1**
adopts daughter 129
attacked by Catholics 72, 76,
139; by Communists 62, **73**,
76, 87
attends peace conference in
Vienna 99, 136

Sartre's ideas—*cont.*
    attitude on: Algeria 91–2, 100–
        1, **113–17**, 119, **124–9**, 132;
        anti-semitism 44, 47, 55–7,
        81–2, 96, 129, 134–5; Berlin
        102, 135, 154; Christianity
        7–8, 14–15, 47, 61, 66, 72–3,
        85, 97, 122–4; cold war 87,
        107–8; Communism and the
        Communist Party 14, 73–4,
        86, 87, 89–90, 92, 96, 99,
        103–5, 108–10, 127; Cuba
        127–8; Czechoslovakia 83,
        136; de Gaulle 116, 125–6,
        135; Hungary 108–10, 112,
        119; Indochina 112–13; Is-
        rael 134–5; Italy 28, 100–1,
        127; Korea 102–4; Marshall
        Plan 91–2, 102, 109; Russia
        102–3, 105, 108–9; Stalinism
        108–10, 112, 119; Venezuela
        134; Vietnam 113, 124–5,
        129, **133–5**.
    cult of the will 28–9, 53–5, 80,
        116, 122
    defines existentialism 8, 75–6,
        110, 138–9
    edits **La Voix du peuple** 136–7
    education, 24–7
    has mumps 75
    interest in theatre 31, 60–1
        105–7; in cinema 28, 32, 84,
        87
    imagery 28, 37, 41–2, 51–2,
        119–20
    income from books. 90
    loses sight of one eye 13, 52, 62
    military service and experiences
        26, 60, 62
    passion for understanding men
        71
    personal characteristics 28–9,
        31, 33, 39, 84, 99–101
    refuses Nobel Prize for literature
        131–2
    resistance movement 62–3;
        résistentialisme 64
    use of classical myths and

        references 8, 17, 50, 62–3, 77,
            130–1, 133
Sartre's views on: bad faith 53–5,
        68, 118, 120–1; existential
        psychoanalysis 19–20, 69–
        72; fatherhood 17–19, 93–4,
        120–2; liberty 17, 20–1,
        52–5, 57, 59, 63–4, 72–3, 80,
        112, 121–2, 140; literature
        and his own literary career 9,
        21–3, 26–7, 41–2, **76–80**,
        99, 106, 113, 130–2; marriage
        26, 99–100; money and pos-
        sessions 99–100; sex 51–2,
        53–5, 97, 139; students 32,
        135–6, 140; violence 123–4,
        128–9, 132–3, 135–7.
Schweitzer, Albert 8–9
Schweitzer, Anne-Marie 7–23,
        24, 75, 130
Schweitzer, Charles 7–23, 25, 30,
        46, 52, 57, 61, 76, 77, 93, 105,
        106, 115, 117, 121, 136, 138
Shakespeare, William 19, 29, 79,
        92–3
Socrates 50
Stekel, Wilhelm 54
Strachey, Lytton, 33

Tel Quel 43
Temps Modernes, Les 73, **75–
        6**, 77, 78, 86, 95, 102, 108,
        110, 114, 116, 125, 126, 127,
        134, 135, 137
Tintoretto 28
Titian 28
Tolstoy, Leo 79
Troisfontaines, Roger 100

Warnock, Mary 143
Wellington, Duke of 68
Wittgenstein, Ludwig 27, 34, 36
Wodehouse, P. G. 79

Valéry, Paul 68
Varin, René 52
Tennyson, Alfred Lord 79

ISLAM IN THE AFRICAN-AMERICAN EXPERIENCE